THE REAL THING

THE REAL THING

REFLECTIONS ON
A LITERARY FORM

TERRY EAGLETON

YALE UNIVERSITY PRESS
NEW HAVEN AND LONDON

For information about this and other Yale University Press publications, please contact:
U.S. Office: sales.press@yale.edu   yalebooks.com
Europe Office: sales@yaleup.co.uk   yalebooks.co.uk

Set in Adobe Garamond Pro by IDSUK (DataConnection) Ltd
Printed in Great Britain by TJ Books Limited, Padstow, Cornwall

Library of Congress Control Number: 2023947196

ISBN 978-0-300-27429-5

A catalogue record for this book is available from the British Library.

10 9 8 7 6 5 4 3 2 1

For Bernard Sharratt

CONTENTS

Note   *viii*

1   Getting Real   1

2   What is Realism? (1)   32

3   What is Realism? (2)   78

4   The Politics of Realism   100

5   Realism and the Common Life   131

     Endnotes   *147*

     Index   *154*

NOTE

Since realism is a term used of several different art forms, I should point out that my focus in this book is on literature alone. I hope, however, that some of what I have to say has a wider application.

T.E.

1

GETTING REAL

Realism, sympathy and reasonableness

In everyday language, realism means seeing a situation for what it is, without distortion or illusion. The word sometimes carries a hint of resignation: to see things as they are may be to acknowledge that there is nothing much you can do about them. One has therefore, as they say, to be 'philosophical' about the situation – an odd use of the term, which effectively equates philosophy with Stoicism and suggests that wisdom consists of bowing one's knee to the inevitable. Since the inevitable is usually unpleasant, this isn't the most appealing of attitudes. Realistic types are clear-eyed, hard-headed women and men who acknowledge the limits of possibility and don't expect too much of the world. They are the opposite of fantasists and idealists, whose demands are exorbitant and unreasonable. The realist is typically preoccupied with the factual or empirical, though there is an irony to be noted here: the current of philosophy we know as empiricism, which held sway over English thought for some centuries, holds that what we know is not real objects but our ideas, impressions or sensations of them. It is thus not realist at all in the sense of the word now common among philosophers. We shall be looking more closely at this question later.

In the course of her novel *Adam Bede*, George Eliot suspends the narrative in order to offer us some reflections on the literary realism which it exemplifies. In a genially patronising tone, she sees it as involving a wry acceptance of men and women's inability to change: 'These fellow-mortals, every one, must be accepted as they are: you can neither straighten their noses, nor brighten their wit, nor rectify their dispositions . . . it is these people . . . that it is needful you should tolerate, pity, and love'. Non-realism idealises its subject-matter, not least by suggesting that human beings have the power to transform themselves; while realism, in telling it like it is, casts doubt on this capacity. There is a politics implicit in this view. Eliot admires the phlegmatic wisdom of the common people, who pursue their customary ways without any eager expectation that life might change for the better. Yet about a decade before *Adam Bede* appeared, a large number of the common people of Britain were clamouring so militantly for root-and-branch political reform that their superiors lived in perpetual fear of revolution. Perhaps the idealisation is Eliot's own.

In this respect, realism is a post-heroic form. Eliot's finest novel, *Middlemarch*, ends on a note of muted disenchantment: there can be no Antigones or St Theresas in an age of railways and cotton mills. Still, the 'unhistoric' acts of ordinary women and men play a vital role in improving the human condition. Humanity is flawed and imperfect; but by portraying it in all its unloveliness, realist art can persuade us to accept its blemishes rather than bleach them out of sight. In the hands of an Eliot, realism cultivates sympathy and tolerance – though we should keep in mind the very different mentality of Jane Austen, who tartly observes in *Persuasion* that the death of one of the novel's more disreputable characters was a stroke of good fortune for his long-suffering parents.

There are two main ways in which literary realism can foster human sympathy. It can show us how its characters 'live' the world from the inside, so that their actions and attitudes come to make more sense. Or it can widen its focus to include the context in which they lead their lives, refusing to treat their actions in isolation and casting light on the reasons why they behave as they do. In both cases, we are prevented from making purely external judgements on individuals and situations. In combining these two perspectives, realist fiction has an edge over both epic and lyric. Epic presents us with the contexts of actions, but it doesn't allow us much access to the intricacies of the human mind; while lyric is an expression of feeling without much by way of a social environment. The hope, then, is that if we can re-create how people experience reality, while at the same time viewing their actions in a broader perspective, we are likely to be more tolerant of their foibles or even of their crimes. Facts can be freshly evaluated in the light of feelings, and feelings modified in the light of facts. Something like this is what Aristotle means by 'equity' in his account of the law. Equity, he argues, 'bids us be merciful to the weakness of human nature to think less about what (the lawgiver) said than about what he meant; not to consider the actions of the accused so much as his intentions, nor this or that detail so much as the whole story'.[1]

If realism grants us access to the inner drama of subjectivity, it can also report on characters and events in a more objective way. It can light up the world from the viewpoint of a single individual, or it can pull the camera back to reveal a more panoramic view of the human landscape. In this way, it can encompass both feeling and fact, subjectivity and social institution. It can also weigh conflicting claims and balance alternative viewpoints, thus qualifying any too-absolute moral judgement. D.H. Lawrence speaks in *Lady Chatterley's Lover* of the novel as managing the flow and recoil of human sympathy, directing it into places where it has gone dead. In all these ways, the realist novel does not simply involve morality; for a line of authors from George Eliot and Henry James to Lawrence and Iris Murdoch, it is the supreme example of it. The novel is the Bible of an increasingly godless age.

The good-hearted doctrine that a deeper understanding of people breeds a deeper tolerance of them is somewhat suspect. It overlooks the fact that to view actions or individuals in context may show them up as even more repellent than we first imagined. Putting things in context does not always make them more acceptable, or even more intelligible. People who are accused of making offensive remarks often claim that what they said has been taken out of context, but what context would justify 'Drop dead, you despicable piece of donkey dung'? Unless you are quoting, joshing, practising your English, speaking on stage or illustrating the literary device of alliteration, an appeal to context is unlikely to let you off the hook. If you made this remark to someone who was sheltering you from a crazed gunman, the context would compound the offence rather than mitigate it. Besides, there is a whole range of contexts to any human action, and it isn't clear who decides which are most relevant. In a similar way, empathising with others may actually deepen our distaste for them. Feeling your way into the mind of a serial killer, or even a serial liar, may make him seem even more abhorrent than you imagined. Empathy is no basis on which to build an ethics. To identify with someone's plight won't necessarily inspire you to come to their assistance. In fact, if your self has now disappeared into theirs, there is nothing of you left to do so. Ethics is a matter of social practice, not of sentiment. Besides, to 'become' someone else by an act of imaginative sympathy abolishes the distance you need in order to judge them, whereas much realist fiction is a critique of reality, not just a recreation of it.

Realism, resignation and reasonableness would seem to be closely linked. Yet the alliance is surely suspect. There are plenty of situations in which it is realistic to expect an enormous amount. One of the slogans of the student uprising in Paris in 1968, thought up by the critic and novelist Maurice Blanchot, was 'Be realistic: demand the impossible!'[2] It is unrealistic (though not irrational) to expect that we could abolish all hatred and antagonism, but ending the military conflict in Northern Ireland was always a feasible prospect. To tell someone to be reasonable generally means admonishing them to scale down their demands. It usually means something like 'Cool it!', 'Back off!', 'Be moderate!' Yet despite the fact that the *Oxford English Dictionary* gives 'moderate' as a synonym of 'reasonable', this is not what the word 'reason' would have suggested to the more radical wing of the eighteenth-century Enlightenment. Being rational or reasonable for them might well have entailed decapitating the monarch and abolishing the aristocracy. Reason can be a revolutionary force as well as a call for compromise. Seeing things as they are involves seeing how they might be different. It is possible for a status quo to be extreme, and for demands to overthrow it to be entirely reasonable. It was the slave trade that was abhorrent and intolerable, not the reformers' attempts to bring it to an end.

'Rational' and 'realistic' can sometimes be synonymous. It is both rational and realistic to expect that it will rain in Manchester sometime this century. Yet there can also be a difference between the two, depending on the meaning of 'rational'. Abolishing gender inequalities is a rational goal, in the sense of being morally compelling; but there are many places around the globe where it is currently unrealistic, in the sense that one would not expect it to happen quickly or easily. It is rational that the actor Charlie Sheen might be appointed abbot of a Benedictine monastery, in the sense that appointing a tomcat or a can of Diet Coke is not. Sheen is male, of sufficient intelligence for the job, capable of abandoning his flamboyant lifestyle if the alternative was being roasted slowly over a fire, and of an Irish Catholic background to which he might inexplicably revert. But it is not a realistic prospect. It is hard to see it happening next week. Realism deals not only with the actual but with the probable, and Abbot Charlie Sheen falls into neither category.

One cannot speak of people, events or situations as realistic. If 'realistic' means true to life, it makes no sense to say that a road accident is true to life. Representations of it (photographs, newspaper reports and so on) may be realistic, but things themselves are not. Only false teeth can be lifelike. To commend a portrait as realistic is to imply that it is not the real thing. It is therefore to assert both an identity and a non-identity between it and what it illustrates. In this sense, realism involves a kind of irony. To be impressed by the fidelity of a representation we must call to mind what is being represented, which then serves to remind us that what we are impressed by is only an image.

When we talk of realism in literature, we are usually speaking of a certain style of representation, one which strikes us as credible and lifelike. The eighteenth-century author Clara

Reeve writes that the novel's highest task 'is to represent every scene in so easy and natural a manner, and to make them appear so probable, as to deceive us into a persuasion (at least while we are reading) that all is real, until we are affected by the joys or distresses of the persons in the story as if they were our own'.[3] On this view, realism works by empathy, a concept which as we have seen already is not immune to criticism. One does not need to feel someone else's pain in order to feel for them.

Yet how can art be true to life and at the same time be art, which is a matter of shaping and selectivity? Marcel Proust describes art as 'a faithful recomposing of life', but how can you recompose things while remaining faithful to how they appear? Or can you evoke their truth more fully by reconfiguring them? In any case, not everything can be represented. Protons are real, but one cannot dash off a sketch of them. A tingling sensation in the spine is more easily represented in print than in paint. For a Christian, the Resurrection was a real event, but no reputable theologian would claim that you could have taken a photograph of it had you been lurking around Jesus's tomb with your mobile phone at the ready. The Battle of Austerlitz really took place, but there can be no way of representing it which conveys every sword clash and scream of pain. All such realism is an edited version of what it portrays.

Besides, real life is stuffed with surreal or grotesque occurrences, such as awarding the Nobel Peace Prize to a politician (Henry Kissinger) who illegally bombed Cambodia, or the fact that world football has been governed for decades by men who are corrupt to the core. Literary accounts of such scandals might well be dismissed as idle fantasy or blatant sensationalism. It is also true that reality sometimes falls short of what we might reasonably expect of it. It would have been more fitting if Alexander the Great had not been so absurdly short in stature, as some ancient authorities report that he was; but history can be slapdash and negligent, failing to arrange its materials in the most suitable fashion. There are times when its tact, artistic craftsmanship and sense of proportion leave much to be desired, so that art must be called in to compensate for these defects. We must mix our facts with a leavening of fiction if their true significance is to be revealed. Florence Nightingale lived on into the twentieth century, but it might have been more appropriate had she died of fever while nursing the wounded soldiers of Victorian England. As Carol Shields writes in *Larry's Party*, 'History, it seemed to Larry, left strange details behind, mostly meaningless: odd and foolish gadgets, tools that had become separated from their purpose, whimsical notions, curious turnings, a surprising number of dead ends.'

Who or what sets the parameters of realism? Who gets to draw the line between the feasible, the improbable and the inconceivable? One answer to the question, deeply unfashionable in postmodern circles, is: the world itself. There are many possibilities which are ruled out by our physical constitution and material circumstances. It is unlikely, for example, that any human being will live forever – a fortunate limitation, since immortality would almost certainly be a form of hell. At the same time, what counts as realistic is in part a cultural and historical affair. Living to the age of eighty is a realistic expectation these days, as it was not in Shakespeare's time. Some societies take a broader view of what is attainable than others. There are Americans who regard possibility as infinite and treat negativity as though it were a thought crime. The self is mere clay in one's hands – passive, pliable stuff awaiting the imposition of the imperious will. In no other spot on the planet does one hear the exultant cry 'I can be anything I want!' as often as in this compulsively upbeat nation, with its curious blend of hard-headed pragmatism and Romantic idealism. In defeatist Britain, by contrast, reminders to feed the hamster are greeted with cries of despair from those appalled by the sheer enormity of the task.

The infantile fantasy of being whatever you want cannot of course be taken literally. You cannot be a chipmunk, a pot of mustard or a thirteenth-century Mongolian sex worker, and only Judi Dench can be Judi Dench. Neither, however, can the fantasy be true in a broader sense. The tone-deaf do not get to be world-class composers; militant Trotskyists do not become President of the World Bank; and those hapless individuals who are pathologically incapable of either lying or bluffing do not get to be politicians. Desire may be limitless, but achievement is not. As Troilus remarks to Cressida in Shakespeare's *Troilus and Cressida*, 'This is the monstrosity in love, lady, that the will is infinite, and the execution confin'd; that the desire is boundless, and the act a slave to limit' (Act 3, Sc. 2). To hold that anything is possible is usually to regard restraint as inherently negative, a view which caused the ancient Greeks to shudder and look fearfully to the skies. They were aware that such inflated self-belief would earn its calamitous come-uppance, as it may still do in our own day.

Facts and interpretations

Realism seeks to see things as they actually are, the paradigm case of which is acknowledging that we shall die. But seeing things as they are is a more arduous exercise than it sounds. For Friedrich Nietzsche and his postmodern successors, this is because how things are is no way in particular. Reality presents itself to us in a whole number of different guises, depending on our standpoint and on the frame of interests within which we decipher it. Indeed, what we call facts are for Nietzsche simply interpretations. (Since this seems to be a statement of fact, it must itself be an interpretation, a point Nietzsche readily concedes.) The postmodern philosopher Gianni Vattimo brands this form of thought 'nihilistic', since it seems to dissolve the world away, but it is a nihilism he cheerfully endorses.[4]

Most people think that you can judge whether a statement is valid by checking it against the facts. But if the facts are themselves interpretations, all we would seem to be doing is checking one set of interpretations against another. To borrow a couple of analogies from Ludwig Wittgenstein, it would be like buying yourself a second copy of the daily newspaper in order to confirm that what the first copy says is true, or passing money from one of your hands to the other and thinking you have made a financial transaction.

Scientists, along with almost everybody in the local supermarket, tend to appeal to the world itself to decide whether what we say about it is true. If you want to determine whether 'Grass is green' is true, look at an actual patch of the stuff. For Nietzscheans, however, what you see when you look at a patch of grass is itself an interpretation, and a loaded one at that. Our perceptions are informed by bias, habit, interest, desire, assumption, convention and the like. So appealing to something called the world is pointless, since the world comes down to your own partisan version of it. It has nothing to say for itself. It has no opinions on how it is to be represented, and does not intervene in our debates over how best to describe it. Moral thinkers have traditionally argued that values and beliefs should be based on a knowledge of how things are. But if 'how things are' is an illusion, we might simply have to choose these things; and this would fit well with the late-capitalist cult of 'options'. However, if reality has no meaning or value in itself, all choices would seem arbitrary.

They are also equally empty. 'If value is constituted by our desires, simply, as such', writes Sabina Lovibond, 'there can be no objectively valid reason why we should want one thing rather than another; what difference does it make, then, what we choose?'[5] It may follow that the only thing of value is not what we choose but the act of choice itself. What matters is not what I choose, but the fact that it is *I* who choose it. It is a viewpoint common to both existentialism and adolescence. As Charles Taylor writes, 'all options (in this view) are equally worthy, because they are freely chosen, and it is choice that confers worth'.[6] Being a brothel keeper may not be the most virtuous form of life, but at least I opted for it. It is not true, however, that we opt for most of what is central to our lives – whether nuclear war breaks out, how our parents treated us as infants, our genetic make-up, who we fall in love with, our skin colour, our vulnerability to sickness and death, whether we are a psychopath or an easy touch.

Postmodernism is wary of facts, a concern with which it sometimes spurns as 'positivist'. (This, in fact, is a crude caricature of that brand of philosophy.) Facts sound too fixed and definitive, whereas postmodern thought delights in the fluid and provisional. They also sound somewhat tedious. This may cause us to hesitate before coming up with such statements as 'Animals do not like being in pain' or 'There are some gay people in China'. (The latter proposition was vigorously denied by my Chinese guide when I first visited the country in the 1980s.) Yet these are facts, just as it is a fact that Darth Vader came from Bristol. The part was played by an immensely tall actor from that city called David Prowse, whose West Country burr was substituted in the final cut.

Is this a 'brute' fact, though? Not if this means being immune to evidence and argument, or that it is established by infallible methods, or that it can never be disproved. That there are no 'brute' facts, however, is a fact. It does not mean that there are no facts at all, rather as the fact that the world is not run by a conspiracy doesn't mean that there aren't conspiracies. There is a delusion that for an account of the world to be true, it needs to be exhaustive, impartial, value-free, exact in every detail, the only valid account of the subject in question and permanently closed to all revision or refutation. The only problem with this is that no such accounts exist. If you assume that this is what truth means, however, you may well end up rejecting the whole concept as unworkable. In this sense, some nihilists are simply disenchanted absolutists. They assume that if the truth is not blazoned in the skies in luminous Gothic script, then there is no such thing. Or if there is such a thing, then, as the sceptic maintains, it is inaccessible to us.

Even if the world consists simply in a set of interpretations, it does not follow that any old interpretation will do. You might read the novels of Jane Austen as insurrectionary tracts urging the violent overthrow of the English gentry, but it is likely that you would feel a fair amount of strain in trying it on. You would sense the works themselves putting up some resistance to this project, and the Nietzscheans find it hard to explain where this resistance comes from (from other people's interpretations, perhaps). There are times when our claims are confronted by the inconvenient weight of the world's body, and may therefore need to be rejected or revised. Reality is, among other things, what resists our designs upon it. It is not just clay in our all-powerful hands, any more than the human body is just stuff to be shrunk, inflated or scrawled upon. The American philosopher C.S. Peirce describes reality as 'that which insists upon forcing its way to recognition as something *other* than the mind's creation'.[7] There is an element of coercion about it.

To deny that there are facts suggests that what is on the wane in our time is not just this or that piece of reality (crinolines and mutton-chop sideburns, for example) but nothing less than *reality itself*, which in an earlier phase of our civilisation was thought be so sturdy and robust. All the same, it is obvious that some versions of reality are more plausible than others, and only an intellectual would be perverse enough to deny it. As Richard Rorty writes, ' "Relativism" is the view that every belief on a certain topic, or perhaps about any topic, is as good as any other. No one holds this view.'[8] Nobody believes that whistling the national anthem is as effective a cure for cancer as surgery. This is merely the fantasy of those who don't get out enough. In any case, if someone did claim that any viewpoint is as good as any other, they would also be committed to claiming the opposite, since each view would be as valid as the other. Relativism of this kind is a form of inclusivism at the level of the mind. Nobody's opinion must be left out. We would not wish those who call for the poor to be exterminated to feel excluded. It would be to marginalise them. This is not a view shared by the vast majority of people – a fact that ought to worry relativists, who are continually on guard for symptoms of 'elitism'. Not all commonsensical views are to be endorsed; but one should be wary of dismissing beliefs held by immense numbers of ordinary people over immemorial stretches of time, beliefs which arise from their day-to-day traffic with the world. Those who reject value judgements as elitist should note that this is not the attitude of most of the population to the performance of rock groups or football teams.

Postmodernists are right that all knowledge is context-bound and historically specific. Any observation is made from within a certain perspective, and is shaped by certain conventional ways of seeing. But this only poses a challenge to the notion of truth if one assumes that seeing things as they are involves seeing them from nowhere. It does not mean that feminism or medical science are no truer than magic or Scientology. You can compare different versions of reality in order to determine which are more explanatory, as scientists do when they exchange one hypothesis for a more productive one. Critical accounts of *Wuthering Heights* which assume that 'Wuthering Heights' is the pet name Heathcliff gives to Catherine are unlikely to be as illuminating as those which don't. Reports on how it is with the world must submit themselves to certain procedures of logic, evidence, coherent argument, rational criteria, testable hypotheses and the like. These are likely to rule in certain propositions and rule out certain others, at least for the moment. Some evidence might emerge in the future to suggest that the Louvre has been in Kuala Lumpur rather than Paris all along, or that John Milton was only pretending to be blind to win himself a spot of sympathy.

This is not to suggest that evidence and argument will lead you infallibly to correct conclusions. Far from it. The history of science is as much the history of its errors as of its discoveries. For one thing, it is possible to disagree on what counts as logical, rational or strongly evidential in particular contexts, in which case we have to talk it over. Sometimes we may reach agreement, sometimes not. As for correct conclusions, scientists might wrangle for centuries over certain questions without ever establishing the truth of the matter. The quarrel between realists and anti-realists, which we shall be glancing at later, may never be resolved. It is just that if truth is what you are after, procedures guided by logic, evidence and experiment are generally more reliable than opening the Bible at random or peering wistfully into your tea cup. It is a sign of the times that one needs to state anything so obvious. It has also become obvious there is a complicity between postmodern thought and a right-wing contempt for fact, truth, science and rationality.

If none of this is of world-shaking importance when it comes to discussing *Sense and Sensibility*, it matters a lot when it comes to determining whether a certain drug might cause foetal abnormalities. Those who are sceptical of rationality in the former case might not be so eager to discard it in the latter. Not many people are sceptical of truth or reason when it comes to deciding which of their legs should be amputated. Similarly, those campaigners against anti-Semitism who suspect that disinterestedness is always bogus might still prefer for their case not to come up before a judge wearing a swastika armband.

For postmodernists, truth is a question of how we organise the world in order to satisfy our needs and promote our interests.

It is manufactured rather than discovered. It has no foundation in how things are in themselves, since on this view, as we have just noted, there is no such thing. We represent the world in ways which are necessary or convenient for ourselves as a species – ways which help us to master our surroundings and flourish within them. Snails no doubt do the same; but because their bodies are so different from ours, so must their world be. What is true for a snail is unlikely to be true for us, and vice versa. So truth is relative to our practical projects. Whether this claim itself is relative is not easy to decide. The philosopher Hilary Putnam sends up the relativist viewpoint by protesting tongue-in-cheek that 'relativism isn't *true for me*'.[9]

In the more flamboyant outreaches of postmodern thought, truth is even seen as relative to the individual. It is not surprising that this case should flourish in rampantly individualist societies like our own, in which the social sense has progressively withered. It is true for me that Outer Mongolia is a suburb of Stratford-upon-Avon, however false it may be for you and the Outer Mongolians. Both claims are to be respected, since it would be dogmatic and hierarchical to label one of them as 'right' and the other as 'wrong'. To call other people's viewpoints false is to assume an unpleasantly elitist attitude to them. It would also seem to lend our own judgements an unwarranted air of absolute authority. It follows that it is offensive to argue that women have been treated with gross injustice throughout the course of history – not only because it discriminates against those who don't share this opinion, but because it implies that we can know this with reasonable certainty, and certainties are the trade mark of the closed-minded. Instead, there should be something of a free market in truth. Perhaps truth is simply whatever version of the world has triumphed in the course of time in contention with others, rather as Microsoft has gobbled up a number of rival enterprises in its day.

Besides, diversity is generally thought to be desirable in itself, so instead of everyone holding in drearily uniform spirit that torturing the innocent is wrong, why not have some people who maintain the opposite and add a little variety to an otherwise rather humdrum existence? Both parties are entitled to their convictions, just as both are entitled to their private property. If no opinion can be backed by compelling evidence, all opinions are on a level. A good deal of dispute can thereby be avoided, which makes for an easier life for those who govern us. As Simon Blackburn remarks, 'Relativism . . . chips away at our right to disapprove of what anybody says.'[10] It is a way of defusing conflict while at the same time avoiding consensus. Yet consensus of some kind is unavoidable even for disagreement. To be able to differ, we must share some conception of what we are differing over. We are not disputing if I think we are talking about quarks and you think we are discussing Queen Nefertiti.

We determine what is true or false in language, and language is nobody's private property. I may discover some earthshaking truth – say, that Thomas Hardy never clapped eyes on a cow – which is known only to me; but since I can formulate it to myself, it must be in principle communicable to others. Unlike the railways and the water supply, truth cannot be privatised. It is a dialogical affair, involving an appeal to certain shared criteria. In this sense, it is rather like finding out how tall someone is. In his *Philosophical Investigations*, Wittgenstein invites us to imagine someone who exclaims, 'But I know how tall I am!' and places his hand on top of his head. He fails to grasp the fact that height is measured by a common standard. Instead, he is as tall as he is tall. The expression 'it's true for me' is just as empty.

Relativism may also apply to whole groups of people. There are, for example, certain marginal cultures with a distinctive identity of their own, whose values and customs may diverge from ours. They may see the world in ways we ourselves can scarcely imagine; yet they have their own cherished customs and beliefs, which are surely to be respected. One of these groups is known as bankers. At first sight, some of their behaviour (fraud, greed, corruption, barefaced deception and so on) may appear unscrupulous, but who are we to pass such superior judgements on them? From what Olympian standpoint do we decide that reducing large numbers of people to financial ruin is 'immoral'? Bankers are simply individuals who do things differently from the rest of us. If we believe in celebrating a variety of lifestyles, we should surely welcome this fact rather than whine about it. Do we really want a timorously conformist world in which everyone refrains from bankrupting large numbers of other people? Surely diversity is a value in itself. Those who think so should take a look at John Stuart Mill's essay *On Liberty*, which laments the fact that social classes are being levelled on the grounds that difference is thereby being erased. There can be a reactionary pluralism as well as a radical one.

If every culture has different standards of truth, how can they ever communicate, let alone engage in mutual criticism? A Javanese may take Western imperialism to task, but why should this lose us any sleep if we do not share his or her cultural assumptions? As the philosopher Kwame Anthony Appiah argues, this viewpoint 'requires us to define hermetically sealed worlds, closed off from one another, within which everyone is trapped into a moral consensus, inaccessible to argument from outside'.[11] As a cosmopolitan-minded Ghanaian teaching in the United States, Appiah speaks with a certain authority on the question. All cultures may be valid if one is thinking of nations or ethnic communities, but not if one is thinking of paedophiles or the US gun lobby. Inclusivity is not always a virtue.

One should not make a fetish of difference, any more than one should of unity. Some postmodernists are reluctant to acknowledge that other cultures may be in some respects quite like our own because it sounds like a rationale for assimilating them to Western norms. It is, in short, a generous error, like assuming that bank robbers are simply trying to grab in the form of bank notes the love that their parents denied them. Yet all it may do is foist on other people yet another Western conception, this time known as relativism. Generally speaking, human beings have a lot more in common than it is currently fashionable to concede. I may believe that the gods require the sacrifice of thirty bullocks a day, while you may be a card-carrying agnostic, but this does not prevent us from co-operating to save someone from drowning.

As Malcolm Bull remarks, 'the available evidence strongly suggests that there are some linguistic, perceptual, expressive and social characteristics common to all societies, and many others which have developed independently in a wide variety of contexts and are absent only in a handful'.[12] The Nuer or Azande may look at the world differently from Texans and Liverpudlians, but many of the features of reality these tribal people pick out – nightfall, hunger, armpits, laughter, disease – are familiar in Texas and Liverpool as well. Nor must those aspects of their world which deviate from our own be impenetrable to us, unless a great many anthropologists have been lying through their teeth. If we can identify these values and practices in the first place, they can hardly be complete enigmas. Whatever we can know cannot be entirely alien. The true aliens are those who are sitting in our laps right now. In a celebrated essay, the philosopher Donald Davidson rejects the idea that different cultures can have conceptual schemes which are incommensurable with each other.[13]

To deny that we have a world in common at a time when the planet is teetering on the brink of collapse seems peculiarly perverse. If anything has unified the human species, it is climate change and weapons of mass destruction, along with global capitalism. With the invention of nuclear weapons, it became possible for the first time in history for the human species to be annihilated as a whole. Everyone has at least that in common, along with McDonalds and the possibility of seeing their prized possessions swept away by floods.

Why does any of this matter? There is no reason why the concept of truth should be a practical problem for the prosperous middle classes, which is no doubt why some theorists are so cavalier about it. There are others less fortunate, however, who need to know the truth of their condition in order to be free of it. Those who seek political emancipation are likely to require some reliable knowledge in order to do so. They are unlikely to be enthused by the news that their situation is in no way particular, or that the claim that they are being humiliated and ill-treated is simply one version of reality among a host of others. Margarita Simonyan, director of the Kremlin's television channel, has declared that all we have in the way of truth is a host of conflicting narratives. So the charge that Vladimir Putin habitually has his political opponents flung out of six-storey windows is neither more or less plausible than the claim that he is secretly working for the CIA. Any theory of knowledge which does not allow us to state with reasonable certainty that there are gross inequalities of income in the world, or that many thousands of Africans were once taken into slavery, must be treated with deep suspicion. There are thinkers today who insist that women have been burdened and despised throughout history, yet who drape words like 'fact', 'truth' and 'objectivity' in scare quotes. In pulling the rug out from under their opponents' notions of truth and objectivity, these authors seem not to notice that they have also pulled it out from under their own.

Cognitive and moral realism

The claim that the world is independent of our thought about it, but that we can have accurate knowledge of it all the same, is known as cognitive realism.[14] The American philosopher Thomas Nagel believes that this form of realism is true, but that it can't be proved.[15] A militant version of the doctrine is proposed by Christopher Norris, for whom

> the universe and all its furniture . . . must be thought not only to exist but also to exert its various powers, properties, causal dispositions etc., irrespective of our various statements and beliefs concerning it. Those statements and beliefs are *true* (objectively so) just to the extent that they pick out real-world objects, processes, or events and just on condition that they predicate the right sort of property.[16]

We shall see in the next chapter the bearing of this argument on literary realism.

To be a cognitive realist is not necessarily to sign on for some fiction of absolute truth. Nor is it to capitulate to a belief in raw facts, or to the myth that our perceptions are free of prejudice. Neither need we assume that the world is only one specific way at any given time, or that the only valid view of it is the view from nowhere. Even so, realists believe that the way the world is doesn't come down to our descriptions of it. In their opinion, it is how things stand in reality which determines whether those descriptions are true or false. Truth on this theory is discovered, not constructed, which is not to deny that the mind plays an active role in the process. Reality is not mind-dependent; but what we make of it, how we identify, describe and organise it, which pieces of it strike us as significant and which do not, how we put it to practical use: all of this involves our needs, interests and values, which of course vary from time to time and place to place. As the philosopher Paul O'Grady remarks, 'there is a way things are, but there are multiple ways of theorising about it, or describing it'.[17] Our forms of description are constrained by the way things are. We are not free to 'construct' reality in any way we like. In any case, what is it that we would be constructing? The verb 'constructing' suggests that there is something out there to be fabricated.

Simon Blackburn argues that if our thought did not sometimes reflect bits of the world more or less satisfactorily, the many successes of science would have to be ascribed to a miracle.[18] This is not an argument likely to cut much ice with postmodernists who, like many students of the humanities, tend to be sceptical of science. Ironically, they take the same dim view of it as the old-fashioned humanists they scorn. Yet science in the early modern period could be a radical, iconoclastic enterprise, which is how much postmodern thought would like to see itself as well.[19]

Realism of this kind is a theory of knowledge, but there is a moral version of it as well. This holds that moral qualities are features of the world. Moral judgements are not just ways of registering one's subjective attitude to what people do. They are not neutral descriptions of a situation ('She made off with his money half an hour after the wedding ceremony') plus an approving or disapproving judgement ('Excellent thing to do!'). On this theory, known as emotivism, ethics is just a more sophisticated form of cheering or booing. Nor for the realist are moral judgements to be seen as neutral descriptions with a prescription tied to their tail ('Don't do this sort of thing!'), as in so-called prescriptivism.[20] To call an action 'fraud' is not just to reproach its perpetrator. Nor is it simply a shorthand way of urging people not to do it. It is rather a statement which is descriptive and evaluative at the same time, such as 'This is murder'. As Roger Scruton puts it, 'the description has the force of a condemnation'.[21] Even when this is not the case – when we are either simply stating facts or simply making value judgements – the two activities remain closely related. Stephen Mulhall remarks that 'it is not that statements of fact *are* judgements of value, but rather that both fact-stating and value-judging presuppose the same capacities of human nature – that only a creature that can judge of value can state a fact'.[22]

On this theory, moral qualities are features of a situation in much the same way that something can be puce or oblong.

There are moral facts just as there are material ones. There is such a thing as moral knowledge, a claim which non-realism is out to deny. For the non-realist, there is no such thing as objective moral truth, from which it follows in Lovibond's words that 'no one can tell you that you are mistaken in your moral (or other) values'.[23] It would be like telling them that they were mistaken in their liking for Mars bars. Morality for some non-realists is a matter of taste, opinion, tradition or community norms. Some people are white supremacists while others are not, rather as some people prefer Raphael to Rembrandt. For the moral realist, however, there is only one standard of valid assertion, which is truth; and this applies to both moral and factual claims. 'Moral and evaluative statements,' writes Alasdair MacIntyre, 'can be called true or false in precisely the way that all other factual statements can be so called.'[24] Like descriptions of reality, moral claims are made according to certain shared procedures, which means that they can in principle be rationally justified. Moral reasoning can thus claim parity with scientific reasoning in the sense that it, too, is answerable to public criteria of evidence.

Being rationally justified does not necessarily mean being right. An argument based on evidence which seems rock-solid at the time may turn out to be groundless. It was rational in 1067 to believe that the sun circled the earth. Moral realism does not mean that we are never in doubt about whether an action is right or wrong – simply that when we make such judgements, it is a question of fact which is at stake. We might argue over whether a certain act is murder, manslaughter or self-defence, and never reach a definitive conclusion; but we cannot claim that kidnapping a small child and imprisoning it for years in solitude in a cramped space is wrong for me but not for the Princess of Wales, or wrong among the Californians but right among the Azande.

At the root of all virtuous action lies an attempt to see the situation as it really is. In this sense, ethics and epistemology are finally at one. The classical moral question is not 'What should I do?' but 'What should I do, given the situation?' The facts of the situation may be hard, even impossible, to establish, which is one reason why ethical argument is potentially endless. But this is how the moral question has been framed by a lineage of moralists from Plato to Hegel. It is true that not all thinkers sign on for this case. Perhaps the greatest of modern philosophers, Immanuel Kant, insists that the realm of facts is one thing and the sphere of values is another. We should obey the moral law for its own sake. We should be moral because it is moral to be so.

For the moral realist, however, to act appropriately requires some knowledge of how things are with us. Acquiring this insight may itself require various moral virtues: honesty and tenacity, a capacity for self-criticism, an effort to view the world without self-interest or self-delusion, a refusal to foist our own private fantasies upon it and so on. In fact, truth itself was originally a moral concept. The word is related to 'troth', which means faith or loyalty. We try to be faithful to the way things are, rather as we pledge our fidelity to someone else. We may also need a degree of intellectual courage in order to confront the ugly and inconvenient, as well as an acceptance of the recalcitrance of things and an openness to their reality. All this is what is meant by objectivity. It is the opposite of self-centredness. Realism of this kind is a moral labour, not a spontaneous impulse. One might claim that it comes a lot less naturally to us than illusion. One advocate of such selfless objectivity is Goethe, not least in his *Italian Journey*. In fact, he is one of the founders of modern literary realism.

So objectivity is not always a bloodless, clinical affair, and disinterestedness is not invariably a cloak for self-interest. On the contrary, they may demand unusual reserves of courage, truthfulness and conscientiousness in their attempts to excavate the truth. One can have a passion for objectivity, as with those investigative journalists in search of foolproof evidence to expose some atrocity. Friedrich Engels admires the way in which Honoré de Balzac, despite his personal sympathies for the French nobility, never ceases to satirise them in his fiction.[25] Against his own inclinations, his artistic integrity compels him to confront them in all their distasteful actuality. Realism, as the narrator of *Middlemarch* observes, represents a 'sturdy, neutral delight' in things as they are, a comment which blends emotional engagement with intellectual impartiality.

Knowing what is good, remarks Iris Murdoch, demands 'a refined and honest perception of what is really the case, a patient and just discernment and exploration of what confronts one'.[26] Goodness, in a word, involves realism; and realism in turn requires a disciplined selflessness which is not far from love. In the end, Murdoch writes, it is only 'to the patient eye of love' that reality reveals itself.[27] Art, she believes, is exemplary of this condition, in which true knowledge and moral value are hard to distinguish. Otherwise we remain mired in the self-serving fantasies which are the ego's natural condition. On this view, most everyday consciousness is false consciousness. 'All is vanity', Murdoch comments, a touch melodramatically. 'The only thing which is of real importance is the ability to see it all clearly and respond to it justly which is inseparable from virtue.'[28] Her own attempt to do so took the form of writing fiction. Those who can transcend the ego through a self-oblivious attention to reality can acknowledge things and persons for what they are, and this in itself is a moral act. 'The realism of a great artist,' Murdoch contests, 'is not a photographic realism, it is essentially both pity and justice.'[29] To which one might add: humility.

There is another sense in which realism may have moral implications. Because it is the literary form most intimate with everyday life, it has the potential to influence that life more decisively than most other literary modes. Emile Zola viewed his work as a novelist as nothing less than the transformation of society, comparing it to that of a surgeon cutting out infections from the social body. The socially reformist zeal of Charles Dickens is legendary. Other Victorian novelists – Charles Kingsley and Elizabeth Gaskell, for example – saw it as part of their task to bring the underworld of the industrial proletariat to the attention of the respectable middle classes, in the generous-hearted misconception that class antagonism was largely the upshot of misunderstanding. For the Marxist critic György Lukács, whose views on realism we shall be considering later, realism is 'not a substitute for political action; it is the structure of consciousness that accompanies it'.[30]

Finally, it is worth noting that literary realists do not have to be moral or epistemological realists as well. You can insist that the world is independent of our descriptions of it while producing an art of pure fantasy. Or you can claim that it is we who determine the so-called nature of things while coming up with some powerfully realist fiction. An author may regard moral values as subjective value judgements, or see them as no more than exhortations to virtue, yet write with impressive moral depth and intricacy. Realism is a family of concepts, and like many a family they do not always see eye to eye.

2

WHAT IS REALISM? (1)

Realism, idealism and the middle class

The term 'realism' seems to have entered the English language in 1853, as a way of describing the fiction of Honoré de Balzac. The critic M.A.R. Habib summarises the form as one which aims for objectivity and direct observation, makes use of accurate descriptive language, generally prefers contemporary experience to the past, adheres to the possible or probable and typically avoids the use of high-pitched rhetoric in favour of simpler, more colloquial idioms.[1] That last point needs qualifying, since the language of realist works can be as dense and figurative as the poetry of *Paradise Lost*. Realism is not always synonymous with plainness. For the most part, however, it is a sober, no-nonsense affair, hostile for the most part to the stylised art of an older, more aristocratic social order. It is the favoured form of a middle class which is for the most part at ease with its world, and which enjoys contemplating its own face in the mirror of the art that it produces. It tends to be wary of the Romantic and idealistic, the mannered and elaborate, the fanciful and fabulous. As George Eliot writes, realism involves 'a humble and faithful study of nature', one which substitutes 'definite, substantial reality' for 'vague forms, bred by imagination on the mists of feeling'.[2] For many nineteenth-century readers, this humble study of nature proved too much to take. The term 'realism' came to suggest the sexually scandalous and morally indecent, and realist fiction joined socialism and anarchism as a menace to bourgeois civility. The fact that it was associated with frivolous, free-loving France blackened its reputation even further.

Definitions of realism are by no means watertight. One might claim that there is very little 'pure' or unadulterated realism, at least until the late nineteenth century. Henry James marks a major turning point here, though even his fiction is haunted by corpses which won't lie down. For the most part, realist fiction is a strikingly hybrid form. From Balzac's criminal genius, Vautrin, to the spontaneous combustion of Krook in Dickens's *Bleak House* or the murder of Jude Fawley's children in Hardy's *Jude the Obscure*, a good many realist works contain patches of non-realism which stretch the reader's credulity well beyond breaking point. Plenty of fictional protagonists seem to have strayed onto the realist stage from myth, epic or romance.

Take, for example, the novels of Charles Dickens. Dickens is praised for painting an incomparably vivid portrait of

Victorian England, yet many of his characters are scarcely of the kind you would run into in a dentist's waiting room. They are freaks and eccentrics who seem to live in the interstices of each other's lives, bouncing off one another like snooker balls, their conversation less a matter of dialogue than of interlocking monologues. It is a distinctively urban form of perception, very different from the way we regard our neighbours in a tight-knit rural community. This is an art bred *by* the city – loud, brash, dynamic, flamboyant – not simply an art about it. It is urban in form as well as content. To this extent, Dickens's fiction is a form of realism – but a form of realism appropriate to new social conditions, as the shocks, collisions, incongruities and random encounters of an urban landscape become the everyday experience of a growing sector of the British population, transmitting their irregular rhythms in the vibrancy of his prose.

There is another sense in which what might appear non-realist in Dickens's fiction might be seen as realistic at a deeper level. His novels are notoriously laced with blatantly engineered coincidences, as when Oliver Twist on the run in London ends up by sheer accident in the household of his own blood relations. In later works like *Bleak House* and *Great Expectations*, however, apparently chance convergences of this kind can signify how characters who seem locked in their own solitary worlds may in fact be deeply enmeshed with each another. Plot can now be a means of bringing to light the mutual debts, bonds and obligations which lie beneath the surface of a fragmented society. True realism delves deeper than appearances. We shall be seeing more of this aspect later.

In his classic study *The Rise of the Novel*, Ian Watt argues that the realist vision displays two pre-eminent features. It refuses what it sees as the false poetic idealism of Romantic and neo-classical art, and it champions 'low' or commonplace subjects over noble or heroic ones.[3] As Watt has fun in pointing out, Defoe's Moll Flanders is a thief, his Roxana is a woman of 'easy virtue', Samuel Richardson's Pamela is a hypocritical serving maid and Fielding's Tom Jones is a fornicator.[4] As for false idealism, a good deal of realist fiction is devoted to exposing delusions and shattering fantasies against the hard rock of reality. It is an art of unmasking and debunking. It also takes a consuming interest in the individual, whom it ranks over the universal, and unlike previous art forms charts the evolution of characters over time. It is notably more specific about the significance of time and place than most earlier literature, and offers the reader what purports to be an authentic account of people's lived experience. Its prose is generally plainer than that of most traditional literary genres, though we have seen already that this claim needs to be qualified. It may be prepared to sacrifice a degree of stylishness to an air of reality. It is the kind of writing which some poststructuralist critics call 'readable', meaning *too* readable, too easily consumed, too apparently unaware that it is as much an artefact as the Pindaric ode or the heroic couplet. 'The [realist] writer's exclusive aim,' Watt comments, 'is to make the words bring his object home to us in all its concrete particularity, whatever the cost in repetition or parenthesis or verbosity.'[5] A character in Henry James's 'The Story in It' remarks that she reads mostly French novels, 'French' being code for realist ones, since 'I seem with it to get hold of more of the real thing – to get more life for my money.'

In their Preface to *Lyrical Ballads*, Wordsworth and Coleridge write that the aim of the volume is to choose 'incidents and situations from common life, and to relate or describe them, throughout, as far as was possible in a selection of language really used by men'.[6] Among other things, the statement suggests a provincial distaste for the upper-class establishment. This bias towards the popular and unembellished may be one reason why realism has thrived so vigorously in the United States, with its lack of a court and aristocracy, its Puritan dislike for the affected and artificial, its tough-minded insistence on telling it like it is, its prizing of a rugged integrity over an effete artistry. To the Puritan mind, fiction, like irony, is too close for comfort to lying, and to compensate for this vice should be as plain-spoken as possible. The word 'fiction' comes to us from a Latin term meaning 'to feign', so that there is a sense in which the term 'realist fiction' is a contradiction in terms.

Realism is also averse to myth, romance and fantasy, along with the miraculous, metaphysical, poetical, melodramatic and supernatural. As we shall see later, it may plunder such materials from time to time, but for the most part it trades in more secular, quotidian stuff, which is exactly what some avant-garde thinkers see as amiss with it. In the eyes of the Surrealist artist André Breton, realism gives vent to 'the intractable mania that consists in reducing the unknown to the known, to the classifiable'. It is a timorous refusal of the innovative and imaginative, cravenly sacrificing the possible to the actual and in doing so consecrating the status quo.[7] T.S. Eliot speaks witheringly of art which strives for an exact likeness to reality as a 'desert'.[8]

By and large, realism is a product of the middle class. Harry Levin sees it as asserting the 'predominance of citizen over courtier'.[9] It educates its readers in new habits of feeling, challenging traditional values and cultivating new ones in their place. It thus plays a vital role in what one might call the middle-class cultural revolution, helping to produce a new kind of self-dependent, self-determining human subject.[10] It is no surprise, then, that this vulgar, upstart form of writing, which has to wait for some time before being graced with the title of literature, turns recurrently on money, property, land, marriage and inheritance. Engrossed by the individual, it explores complex psychological states beyond the reach of epic or romance. Because the middle classes are for the most part concerned less with the traditional than with the here-and-now, realism is distinguished from other literary currents by its sense of the contemporary. The word 'novel' derives from the Latin for 'new'. Events are represented as being vividly present, in both senses of the word. The eighteenth-century novelist Samuel Richardson pushes this to an absurd extreme in *Pamela*, a novel in which the chaste heroine, who is forever jotting down her experiences as they happen, writes to tell us that her lecherous master is climbing into bed with her at this very moment. Yet if realist fiction is a reflection of middle-class civilisation, it is also a critique of it. From Stendhal to Martin Amis, it feels free to take the status quo to task. It can be mercilessly satirical of its masters and profoundly disillusioned with their lowbrow way of life.

Realism, then, has a historical basis. Roughly speaking, epic belongs to a heroic era, romance to the medieval age of chivalry and the realist novel to modern times. Its high point is the nineteenth century, when it was to become for the first time in history the dominant literary form. In *The Communist Manifesto*, Marx lavishes praise on the middle classes (the most potent revolutionary force in history, he argues) for their clear-eyed vision of the world, their refusal to idealise it out of existence. They have 'drowned the most heavenly ecstasies of religious fervour, of chivalrous enthusiasm, of philistine sentimentalism, in the icy water of egoistic calculation . . . The bourgeoisie has stripped of its halo every occupation hitherto honoured and looked up to with reverent awe.'[11] It is one of the great backhanded compliments of nineteenth-century Europe. Bourgeois realism is the enemy of sentimental cant and pompous pageantry. In what Marx regards as a historic breakthrough, it seeks to tell it like it is, ugly and brutal though it may be. In Sancho Panza-like spirit, the middle classes pride themselves on their robust common sense, in contrast to the privileged, Don Quixote-like fantasies of their social superiors. In their stoutly empiricist way, they believe in what they can touch and taste, not in idle abstractions.

Marx's judgement is by no means entirely positive. If the bourgeoisie are opposed to ritual and florid rhetoric, it is partly because they are philistine and acquisitive to the core, more concerned with the state of the marketplace than the state of their souls. They are materialists in both the positive and negative senses of the term, as the ambivalent tone of Marx's comments would suggest. Even so, though the capitalist class may be a predatory bunch, they are insolently upfront about the fact, substituting 'naked, shameless, direct, brutal exploitation' for those forms of oppression which are 'veiled by religious and political illusions'.[12] Better an unabashed slave-driver than one brandishing a Bible.

Realism combines a trust in the solidity of social existence with a sense of its instability. It thus corresponds to two conflicting aspects of middle-class society. If its moral values are those of prudence, decency and sobriety, its social and economic life is a question of risk, struggle and endless enterprise. If the bourgeois is a stolid, respectable fellow at home, he is a swashbuckling captain of industry in the public sphere. It is thus that the realist novel manages to embed itself in everyday life without courting the danger of dullness. There is nothing dull about bankruptcy or being a billionaire. Realism therefore exerts a double fascination: over those timorous, home-loving souls who console themselves with images of the familiar, but also over those buccaneering types who are inspired by danger, adventure and constant striving. Both personas may inhabit the same breast.

The middle class, however, has a problem with order and closure. There is no gracefully symmetrical shape to a market economy, and no natural end to the acquisition of property. On the contrary, accumulation must be incessant if you are not to go under. (It is worth noting that the word 'real', which derives from the Latin *res* (thing), was originally a legal term denoting immutable property, a meaning which lives on today in the phrase 'real estate'.) No author illustrates this 'bad infinity' of accumulation (as Hegel would call it) more than Daniel Defoe, in whose novels entrepreneurship is as openended as the process of narration itself. Piling up wealth can go on forever, and so can telling stories – an activity which has itself become by this time an eminently saleable commodity on the market. Having achieved a degree of affluence and contentment, Defoe's characters tend to launch out again almost instantly on fresh adventures, plunging headlong into yet more gambles and hazards. This means that there is no natural closure to this author's novels. Their endings generally feel arbitrary and provisional, more of a cut-off than a conclusion. Ungratified desire is the natural condition of humanity, as the protagonist skids from one sexual partner, domestic set-up or shady commercial venture to the next. Nothing is more volatile than money, which turns the whole of human existence into one endless escapade. Money and fantasy, the most mundane and improbable of phenomena, go logically together.

There is a self-contradictory ring to the phrase 'literary realism'. 'Realism' suggests the gritty and unadorned, even the caustic and abrasive, whereas literature is a question of artistry – of the chicanery of form, the artifice of style, the consoling cheat of a happy ending and the like. 'Realist fiction', as we have noted, sounds even odder, since fiction is not real in the sense that having your teeth extracted is. In fact, the word 'fiction' first emerged when literature was becoming gradually more realist, in order to indicate that such writing was not the real-life report one might mistake it for. There would be no need for such a label if all literary works read like *Alice in Wonderland*. Fredric Jameson finds a similar strain in the phrase 'representation of reality'.[13] This is partly because we think of representations as having only a secondary reality, in which case it is hard to see how they can capture the opulence and density of the world. But it may also seem an odd expression because you can claim that reality is itself a set of representations, as opposed to a collection of brute facts. We have looked at this question already in our discussion of realism and anti-realism.

Some realist writing wants to break out of the literary sphere altogether in order to confront the world eyeball-to-eyeball; yet this itself is a literary device. Writing which aims to give us reality in the raw is the most realist; but it is also the least realistic, since in any absolute sense this is impossible. The homespun language of Wordsworth and Coleridge's *Lyrical Ballads* is a smack at literary conventions (those of the neo-classical verse of the eighteenth century), but it is really a shift from one set of conventions to another, not from convention to real life. Perhaps, then, there is a touch of bad faith about all realist writing, which aims to convince us that it is the real thing yet knows that it isn't, and knows that the reader knows this as well.

There are critics who regard realism as a universal category – indeed, as the foundation of all authentic art, whatever its time or place. We shall be looking at this argument later in the work of György Lukács and Eric Auerbach. Alternatively, you can see it as the product of a specific historical period, say from Jane Austen and Walter Scott to the present day, with one or two notable precursors such as *Don Quixote* and the fiction of the eighteenth century. As a form, it has proved remarkably difficult to dislodge. After the modernist revolution in the arts, it resumed pride of place in the literary pecking order, at least in the English-speaking world, without much sense that anything especially outlandish had just happened. There were, to be sure, writers on whom modernism left an indelible mark, and many of its motifs were to return in postmodern guise. Even so, Philip Larkin appeared on the scene as though T.S. Eliot had never existed. For some anglophone authors, normality had been thankfully resumed, after a brief encounter with the off-beat and aberrant.

You can also see realism as a mode of writing which is confined neither to a specific time, place or genre but which weaves its way in and out of all sorts of works over the centuries. You may come across patches of realist writing in some ancient texts, mixed in with other modes, or in contemporary works of fantasy and science fiction. There are similar anticipations of modernism. Nor is realism restricted to fiction. The Roman poet Horace recommends artists to 'examine the model of human life and manners as an informed copyist and to elicit from it a speech that lives'.[14] Poets, he insists, must base their inventions on what is commonly recognised.

So realism is by no means confined to prose or to the modern period. We can speak of realist poetry, such as Chaucer's *Canterbury Tales*, Wordsworth's 'Michael' or Tennyson's 'Enoch Arden'. If the form is hard to pin down, it is partly because what counts as realist is culturally variable. Say we were to stumble across a literary work from some ancient civilisation which portrayed couples who have freckled children being buried up to their necks on the seashore as the tide comes surging in. Perhaps we might take this at first as some weird piece of surrealism. Further anthropological research, however, might reveal that the society in question really did visit such penalties on those guilty of producing offspring whose freckles were regarded as blemishes displeasing to the gods, in which case we would be forced to reclassify the text as realist. Even within the same culture, as Roman Jakobson reminds us, a work intended as realist by the author may not be received in the same way by a reader.[15] The opposite is possible as well. The eighteenth-century bishop who threw his copy of Swift's *Gulliver's Travels* impatiently into the fire, complaining that he didn't believe a word of it, was reading a non-realist work through a realist optic.

So you cannot always tell whether a work of art is realist simply by inspecting it. You might need to know more about the customs and convictions of the society which produced it – what it considers to be unremarkable, mildly improbable, utterly fantastic and so on. It would also be worth knowing what it regards as appropriate for art to represent. Someone who is carried out of the theatre giggling uncontrollably at the death of Cordelia in *King Lear* may be operating under different cultural conventions from our own. Perhaps they hail from a culture in which presenting death on stage is so incongruous as to stir them to incredulous laughter. In this sense, realism is for the most part a function of the relation between a literary text and its social context, rather than a set of intrinsic features. I say 'for the most part' because it is hard to see how any civilisation could regard as realist a work of art in which everyone has eight limbs apiece. Even so, if our own civilisation undergoes a sufficiently cataclysmic change in the future, quite a lot of what happens in science fiction might turn out to be as true to life as *EastEnders*.

Realism can mean being faithful to the material world, or being faithful to the way it is experienced. As with Leopold Bloom's interior monologues in James Joyce's *Ulysses*, or the reveries of Virginia Woolf's Mrs Dalloway, one can chart the intricate motions of the inner life with the same plausibility that one can bring to descriptions of the plumbing in the Pompidou Centre. In a much-discussed essay entitled 'Modern Fiction', Woolf clearly considers her own work to be more realist than that of down-to-earth, plain-speaking authors like Arnold Bennett, H.G. Wells and John Galsworthy, whose true-to-life narratives she regards as mechanistic and superficial.[16] On this view, plot, probability, credible characters and the rest of the realist baggage are distractions from the real truth about women and men, which is inward rather than external. The real for Woolf is essentially psychological, rather as for Marcel Proust the subjective impression is the criterion of truth.

One might note, however, that this opposition between inner and outer worlds is ripe for deconstruction. Subjectivity itself is constituted by our relations with others and with the world. We are born human, meaning we belong to a specific species of animal, but being a person is something we have to become through our dealings with others. In any case, in what sense is material reality 'external' to human consciousness? Would we say that our siblings or cheese sandwiches are 'external' to us? Doesn't it just mean that they are separate entities from ourselves? Perhaps it makes sense to speak of 'external' reality if one thinks of the self as an immaterial soul peering out at its surroundings from somewhere deep inside the body. It makes less sense if one thinks of the self as an agent bound up with the world. Only a contemplative mind is likely to experience one's wristwatch or one's grandmother as 'out there'.

In Woolf's view, the realm of feeling and sensation is more real than sanitation reports or inventories of furniture. What one might broadly call psychology cuts deeper than the prosaic sphere of garbage collection and parking tickets. This is a particularly popular conviction among those whose environments are fairly unpleasant, not least in urban and industrial society. No doubt it would have come as a surprise to Homer or Goethe. Yet psychology is undercut in its turn by psychoanalysis. Reality for psychoanalytic theory is not identical with everyday consciousness. One does not grasp what is real simply by turning inwards. Rather, the Real is human desire, not least the unconscious desire for oblivion which Freud names the death drive. It is an implacably impersonal force which disrupts the order of everyday meaning – a crippling lack or non-being which we stuff with fantasies of one kind or another in order to fabricate what we call everyday life. And this includes the flux of human consciousness. The function of this customary world is to mask the Real rather than disclose it. Because desire is absolute and unconditional, incapable of being satisfied by any actual object, it is blatantly unrealistic in its demands.

Such is the case with Shakespeare's Othello, whose pathological sexual jealousy plunges him into an ontological crisis in which run-of-the-mill reality is struck hollow. It becomes a set of flimsy surfaces concealing some dreadful abyss of non-being. The void in question is literally a nothing, since Othello's partner Desdemona has not in fact been unfaithful to him; but in the protagonist this negativity assumes palpable form, swelling to paranoid proportions as the Real lays bare the fraudulence of the familiar. Leontes of *The Winter's Tale*, a character as insanely mistrustful of his wife as Othello himself, feels much the same:

> Is whispering nothing?
> Is leaning cheek to cheek? Is meeting noses?
> Kissing with inside lip? . . .
> Why, then the world and all that's in't is nothing;
> The covering sky is nothing; Bohemia nothing;
> My wife is nothing; nor nothing have these nothings
> If this be nothing.
>
> (Act 1, Sc. 2)

The most trivial phenomena of daily life are a brazen-faced denial of the horror which lurks beneath them. There is a crack or flaw in everyday reality which yields Othello and Leontes a terrifying glimpse of utter vacuity. For those afflicted by such paranoid jealousy, the world is both drained of significance and stuffed too full of it, so thickly coded and insistently meaningful that the slightest word or gesture lends itself to being obsessively over-interpreted.

For psychoanalytic theory, then, the Real is fantastic to its core. Indeed, our chief access to it is through those routine fantasies we call dreams. Psychoanalysis places little credence in the world of kid gloves and fishing tackle. Truth in its view is outlandish and uncanny, an affront to the pragmatists and purveyors of common sense. Its home is a non-place remote from daily existence known as the unconscious. There is, to be sure, such a thing as common reality, but we can cope with it only by the exercise of force. What Freud calls the reality principle fashions a stable environment for the ego only by repressing the turbulent pleasure principle; and it is the need to work, he suggests, that makes this repression imperative.[17] Otherwise we would simply lounge around the place all day in various postures of erotic bliss. The ordinary world is not in Freud's view the most pleasant of places to be. There is a sense in which it is not natural to humanity. What is natural to us is a certain delectable indolence. Though we inhabit the conventional world as a fish swims in the ocean, it is not really our kind of thing.

Realism, reality and representation

We have seen that for realist philosophers the world is independent of our accounts of it. For anti-realists, by contrast, the accounts we accept as true are just what we mean by 'the world'. If we look at literary realism in this context, it turns out to be peculiarly paradoxical. Realist fiction appears to describe persons and events which exist independently of it. We are supposed to make believe that David Copperfield is a real-life person undergoing real-life adventures.[18] In this sense, literary realism resembles the realism of the philosophers. It, too, posits a real world which is not reducible to whatever we have to say about it. Yet the form is in fact an illusion. The statement 'In the second half of the 1960s I travelled repeatedly from England to Belgium', which is the opening sentence of a novel by W.G. Sebald, is supposed to represent an actual state of affairs, but the reader knows that this is not the case. Even if the author did in fact travel repeatedly from England to Belgium in the 1960s, this is irrelevant to what he is doing here. Sebald's sentence, whether it happens to be true or false, is part of the fictional world he is constructing. Since we are aware that this is a novel, we know that we are not meant to take the remark as a piece of autobiographical information even if we happened to have accompanied the author on his trips to the Continent. Someone might protest that an author who has actually lived through what he or she writes about will come across as more authentic than one who has not; but *Macbeth* is a gripping piece of drama even if it is doubtful that Shakespeare himself ever ran into three witches or watched his wife go mad. Conversely, there are plenty of authors who write unconvincingly about events they have actually experienced.

So the world of the novel has no existence independent of its descriptions. It is simply all of its portrayals and propositions taken together. It projects an apparent 'outside' to itself, but only by its internal modes of operation. There is no Mansfield Park or Treasure Island distinct from what the novels in question tell us about them. They exist purely in the language which constitutes them. The trick of realism is to make their existence seem independent of that language. There is no actual rift between what is represented and the way it is represented, but we are invited to imagine that there is.

Ironically, then, literary realism is in some ways close to what the philosophers call anti-realism. For the anti-realist, as we have seen, the world comes down to our accounts of it. This is also true of realist fiction, which produces the very reality it appears to replicate. The literary form, which is admired above all others for telling it like it is, is actually a sleight of hand. Or at least it would be did it not come with the tacit instruction, 'You know this isn't true, but make-believe for the moment that it is.' Reading realism thus involves a form of cognitive dissonance: we assent to its reality while knowing that it is fabricated. We are aware that Catherine and Heathcliff have no actual existence as individuals, being no more than patterns of black marks on a set of pages; but these marks are organised in a way which makes it seem that the pair are real people whom *Wuthering Heights* is representing, rather than figments it is manufacturing. Realism is mimetic, or imitative, since it seems to hold up a mirror to the everyday world; but it is also non-mimetic, since what we see in this mirror is its own invention. In some Victorian novels, the supposedly independent existence of characters even seems to carry on beyond the last paragraph of the book ('Their children, as yet unborn, were to think of their sacrifice with tender gratitude, and did honour to their memory by naming their own offspring after them.'). By looking beyond the end of the fiction, you can suppress the fact that it is a fiction at all.

On this view, realism succeeds by denying its own artifice, like a magician who only appears to saw through his blood-soaked forearm. Such works, claims Fredric Jameson, 'seek obsessively to cancel [themselves] as fiction in the first place'.[19] The realist author, writes Guy de Maupassant, 'will have to compose his work in so skilful and concealed a manner, with such apparent simplicity as to make it impossible to perceive and indicate its plan, to uncover its intentions'.[20] Some modernist works of art, by contrast, deliberately draw attention to their own 'constructed' nature, partly to avoid what they see as realism's bad faith in this respect. Realist writing would seem to be a case of art concealing art, which is one reason why it has a particular appeal to the philistine. Those who don't think much of art in general are likely to feel most at home with those forms of it which are as little like art as possible. (The opposite is true of those without much sense of humour, who tend to appreciate only broad forms of it such as farce, slapstick and good clean fun.) Realism is the most unliterary of literary arts – a paradox that underlies one of the first great realist novels, *Don Quixote*. It tends to be more earth-bound and materialist than, say, pastoral, lyric or elegy.

As a mode of investigating reality, realism is also the most cognitive of literary forms. Rather than simply portraying the world, it yields us some intricate knowledge of it. How can this be so, however, if it is a sleight of hand? It is true that it does not represent actual situations, but the situations it does depict are drawn from the stuff of everyday life. It presents us with nothing we could not find there, which is not true of such superb pieces of fantasy as 'The Walrus and the Carpenter' or 'The Teddy Bears' Picnic'.

There is an obvious objection to this argument. Don't realist novels sometimes introduce us to real-life individuals such as Horatio Nelson or Catherine the Great? Don't they inform us (for example) that Sofia is the capital of Bulgaria, that Elizabethan London stank to high heaven and that the paperclip was invented by a Norwegian? Facts such as these may indeed crop up in realist writing, but not exactly as information. Fiction is not just a disguised form of documentation. If it provides us with some empirical truths, it does not do so as an end in itself. The function of such fragments of reality is rather to contribute to the novel's overall way of seeing. We learn that Sofia is the capital of Bulgaria because this is where the hero flees to avoid being arrested. Facts are selected, adapted and assembled in the name of truths which are moral rather than empirical.

A proposition like 'Lok was running as fast as he could' represents a state of affairs, whether it is true or fictional. This is not the case with statements like 'You devious little creep!' or 'How's it going, old pal?', which do not represent anything. We also speak of certain bits of language 'reflecting', 'reproducing' or 'corresponding to' certain bits of reality. All these terms are metaphorical, and whether they illuminate very much is debatable. In what sense, for example, does the word 'guilt' reflect the condition of guilt? Words are not images or reproductions. There may be a social convention to the effect that the word 'guilt' should be taken to denote a certain state of mind, but it is not especially helpful to see this as a reflection or representation.

We sometimes speak of language as representing reality, but this can be misleading. It may lure us into seeing words or concepts as images of things. Concepts, however, are not best thought of as mental pictures. What mental picture do we have when we hear the word 'improbably' or 'irredentism'? You can say that the word 'porcelain' represents a white, vitrified, translucent ceramic object, but what do words like 'maybe', 'Hi there!' or 'Get lost!' represent? Does knowing the meaning of the word 'octopus' involve having an image of an octopus in your head? How do you have a mental picture of 'Diplomatic negotiations are still in progress'? The fact is that we usually understand language without having any mental images at all. Concepts are ways of using words, not reflections of objects. Meaning is a social practice, not in the first place a process in our heads. If you can use the word 'pedunculate' in roughly the same way as your fellow English-speakers, then you have the concept of it. And to have a correct concept of 'pedunculate' is simply to know what it means.

Even in the case of objects, representation is not a simple affair. You could not teach language to a very young child by pointing at a bunch of jellybeans and exclaiming 'Jellybeans!' There is no obvious connection between the sweets and the sound. Anyway, 'Jellybeans!' might mean 'This stuff is poisonous', or 'Leave the orange ones for me'. The child would already have to be initiated into the practice of indicating. It would have to know that a pointing finger is meant to single something out. It would also need to have the concept of naming; to be aware that 'jellybean' is the name (rather than, say, the size or colour) of the sweet; that to know this name signifies a whole class of things rather than just this particular item; to understand that someone is trying to teach it something and so on. A lot of stage setting is necessary for one thing to represent another. To identify a portrait as a likeness of Thomas Jefferson involves grasping how a configuration of matter on a canvas can 'stand for' a real individual. In this case, at least, there is a visual similarity between the representation and what it refers to, but this is not always so. The word 'tortoise' does not look like a tortoise, any more than Members of Parliament resemble the constituents they represent.

The fact that people and situations can be represented – that reality lends itself to being reproduced – is perhaps too readily taken for granted. Despite Henry James's assertion that 'till the world is an unpeopled void there will be an image in the mirror',[21] one might dimly imagine a universe of which this was not true – one in which the looking glass, like Dracula's, is empty. It is as though the fact that they can be captured in paint or print is an inherent property of things. What is real is what is reproducible. Yet there are occasions when representation seems to break down altogether. Such is the theme of James's short story 'The Real Thing', in which a Major Monarch and his wife, an eminently respectable married couple who have fallen on hard financial times, resort with a touch of pathos to offering themselves as models to the portrait artist who recounts the tale.[22] Try as he may, however, the artist proves incapable of making the Monarchs come alive on his drawing board, and is finally forced to dismiss them from his employment. The problem he confronts is two-fold. For one thing, the couple are so stereotypically genteel that they look rather like drawings already. 'She was singularly like a bad illustration', is the artist's mildly malicious comment on the straitlaced Mrs Monarch. They are figures who might have stepped out of the pages of some high society magazine. The pair are 'all convention and patent leather',[23] too hidebound by their meticulous manners to inspire the artistic imagination. They are like stereotypes of themselves, and thus seem too perfect to be real. The real, by contrast, has a certain fuzzy, blemished air about it. It can be identified by its imperfections. James was struck by the way in which English high society, of which he himself was a kind of permanent house guest for many years, resembled a work of art in its mannered, formalised quality; yet this also lent it a brittleness which made it hard for an artist to portray.

On the other hand, the Monarchs resist representation because they are too much the real thing – too stolidly themselves to lend themselves easily to visual recreation. They are like second-rate actors who are incapable of performing what they are. This is unusual, since being yourself usually involves a degree of playacting. 'Now the drawings you make from us, they look exactly like us', the Major enthuses,[24] while the artist murmurs ruefully to himself that this is indeed the problem. Too much reality can be detrimental to realism. It leaves nothing for the creative mind to seize upon. So the Major and his wife are both too substantial, and not substantial enough, to make the mysterious leap from studio to artist's easel. They seem to be constructed purely out of social convention, and thus appear inauthentic; but these conventions are so rigid as to lend them a predictability which leaves no room for imaginative speculation. Either way, the artist can find no foothold.

What the narrator is used to sketching is not so much things themselves, but the capacity of things to become images of themselves. Or, for that matter, images of someone or something else. It is this capability that the Monarchs disastrously lack, in contrast to another of the artist's models, the absurdly named Miss Churm, who as a young working-class Londoner is able to pose as anything from a shepherdess to a Russian princess. When Major Monarch doubts that this 'freckled cockney' looks enough like an aristocrat to be represented as one, the artist replies that she will when he makes her so. Miss Churm, who has 'a curious and inexplicable talent for imitation',[25] is infinitely 'makeable', while the Monarchs are frustratingly intractable.

There is a social aspect to this contrast. It is as though Miss Churm, being no more than a humble plebeian, is nothing in herself, but precisely for that reason has the knack of morphing into anything at all; while the Monarchs, being the real thing in the social sense of the term, which is to say genuine rather than bogus gentry, might find it beneath their dignity to be anything but themselves. 'She was the real thing,' the artist observes of Mrs Monarch, 'but always the same thing.'[26] Finally sent packing from his studio, the stubbornly non-reproducible couple 'bowed their heads in bewilderment to the perverse and cruel law in virtue of which the real thing could be so much less precious than the unreal'.[27] Their mistake, so to speak, is not exactly that they are realists, but that they are naive realists. They see art simply as a mirror which reflects the truth. The best model for an ageing roué is an ageing roué. This overlooks the fact that art presents things as they are only by an imaginative transformation of them – one which may make them seem even more real than they appear in everyday life.

So there can be no realism without an admixture of illusion. Truth is a matter of what the artist makes of his or her raw materials, not just of fidelity to fact. You can of course simply make a facsimile of something, but what is the point of that? Why do we greet with cries of acclaim a sketch of a banana that looks exactly like a banana? Perhaps because we appreciate the skill with which the object is so faithfully rendered. But then realism becomes simply a question of technique, which is to diminish its significance.

In any case, the reality on which a writer labours is never exactly raw. We shall be returning to this claim a little later. It is the task of classical realism to reveal something of the order inherent in reality, not simply to impose its own capricious design on it. If this can be achieved, the work of art can be both shapely and true to life. Or, to put the point in more traditional terms, you can have beauty and truth together.

Fiction, reflection and make-believe

Things are not much helped by substituting 'reflection' for 'representation'. Writing of a commentary by Lenin on Leo Tolstoy, the critic Pierre Macherey agrees with Lenin's claim that Tolstoy's work holds up a mirror to the Russian revolution of 1905.[28] Yet this mirroring, Macherey argues, is a complex affair, by no means a direct reflection of the world as it stands. If literary works are in some sense mirrors, they are mirrors marked by flaws and blind spots. In fact, they are as significant for what they don't reflect – for their exclusions and distortions – as for what they do. There are things which do not and cannot figure in the mirror – in the case of Tolstoy, certain contradictions in society of which he could not be conscious. Even so, the mirror makes us aware of these absences, which thus become dimly present. It is as though it allows us to see more clearly what isn't there. There is also no reason to assume that what we see in the mirror must form a coherent whole. On the contrary, it may be fragmentary and discordant. 'The mirror is doubtless defective; the outlines will sometimes be disturbed; the reflection faint or confused', remarks George Eliot in *Adam Bede*, reproaching the kind of naive realism which holds that art (or mirrors) always tell it like it is. A mirror offers us a version of reality, but it does so from a viewpoint which cannot be captured in the mirror itself. And because this viewpoint is invisible to us, we might be tempted to take it as beyond question. In complicating the idea of art as mirror, however, the metaphor comes apart in Macherey's hands. A mirror with flaws, blind spots, fragmentary images and distorting perspectives doesn't sound the most reliable sort to comb your hair in.

To see literary works as representations is to risk dematerialising them. Rather than existing in their own right, they are reduced to mere copies of something else. The work's power is derived purely from what it portrays. Its truth lies outside itself. Plato was suspicious of art because it struck him as a pale reflection of a thing, which was in turn a pale reflection of an Idea. The Russian painter Kazimir Malevich, by contrast, thought of his abstract canvases as realist because they were material phenomena in themselves, rather than images of what lay outside the frame. A Constructivist rocking chair does not represent a rocking chair. It is a chunk of reality, not a reading of it. A Dadaist spectacle is non-representational. So is a juggler or a trapeze artist. It might be claimed that these things represent themselves, but this is a curious way of speaking. Just as Donald Trump is the only person in the world who cannot in principle look like Donald Trump, whereas some other luckless souls always might, so material objects cannot be said to resemble themselves. There is no more useless proposition, remarks Ludwig Wittgenstein in his *Philosophical Investigations*, than the identity of a thing with itself. On this estimate, the most realist kind of art represents nothing at all. The less works reflect the material world, or the 'inner' sphere of emotions, the more solid they become. Art is free only when it is not enslaved to realms beyond itself.

Free from the burden of conforming to a world outside it, non-realist art can turn instead to the business of exploring its own material existence. It can also allow the imagination freer rein. A photograph can show us a cathedral constructed of marble, but a poem or novel can portray one built entirely out of marble and entirely out of mustard. Characters in non-realist fiction can be in six different places at once, which in real life is true only of the ubiquitous philosopher Slavoj Žižek. Whereas the realist work assumes that it is underwritten by reality itself, non-realist art draws its authority purely from itself. The price it pays for this autonomy, however – angst, isolation, arbitrariness, dysfunctionality – is a steep one.

Representation has a history, both in art and life. You can reproduce reality only according to certain rules and acquired ways of seeing, and these vary from one time and place to another. A specific way of framing reality is what the art critic Ernst Gombrich calls a style, which in his view 'rules even where the artist wishes to reproduce nature faithfully'.[29] As Northrop Frye puts it, 'when the public demands [of painting] likeness to an object, it generally wants the exact opposite, likeness to the pictorial conventions it is familiar with'.[30] It is true that the realist novel is governed by fewer conventions, than, say, a Petrarchan sonnet, and that these conventions are less obtrusive than they are in most other works of art. In fact, the novel has been described as a form without rules. The more it evolves, the fewer social and artistic restraints there are on what it can handle, until in our own time it can deal with pretty much anything you like.

Yet the whole business of make-believe is a practice which we have to learn. When we open a realist novel, a complex set of literary conventions moves spontaneously into place, such as 'these events are mostly fictitious, but you are supposed to make believe that they are real without actually believing that they are'; 'you are not supposed to ask how the anonymous narrator came to know all this'; 'you are not to waste your time worrying about whether some of this actually happened in real life'; 'you are not expected to do anything practical as a result of reading this text, as you would with a notice reading "This End Up"'; 'you are invited to take this not just as a particular narrative but as in some way illustrative of more general truths' and the like. Without these tacit instructions, we would be baffled to know how to proceed. We also acknowledge that what we are about to read is the product of certain techniques which do not draw attention to themselves. In fact, we may admire the skill and discretion with which such techniques are concealed, rather than assume from their invisibility that the novel was written by reality itself.

The styles or vocabularies of which Gombrich speaks allow an artist to pose certain questions while ruling out certain others. The artist 'needs a vocabulary before he can embark on a "copy" of reality'.[31] He cannot just open his eyes and take a look. This is equally true of everyday life. We always perceive the world under some description or other. We could make no sense of what we see unless we were able to bring a range of concepts and assumptions to bear on it; and the primary medium of these is language. When an author writes or a painter paints, they shape their material, often unconsciously, according to a set of artistic conventions – conventions that may be so coercive that to write or paint differently would be inconceivable. So much is commonly accepted. What is less often underlined is that the material an artist shapes is already meaningfully organised. Our experience of the world is not just one of a swarming chaos awaiting the imposition of artistic form, as some modernists tend to imagine. Reality has a rough-and-ready structure before the artist comes to lay hands on it, though it is not one that he or she is obliged to reproduce. The world comes to the artist, as to the rest of us, already baptised, granted a name and identity. It is carved up conceptually in a range of ways. Caught up in a mesh of meaning, the world is always already significant. Rachel Bowlby reminds us that 'our reality is already, in large measure, a representational one, both verbally and visually'.[32]

What Gombrich calls styles cannot be spoken of as true or false, any more than you could speak of Swedish or Swahili as true or false. A language can generate true or false propositions, but it cannot be true or false in itself. A picture, Gombrich remarks, 'can be no more true or false than a state-

ment can be blue or green'.[33] This, however, needs some qualifying. Ways of seeing may not be true or false in themselves,
but they may involve beliefs and assumptions which are. Even
so, it is not true or false to shake hands, allot soliloquies to
porters as well as princes or have only a certain number of
characters on stage at the same time. Shaking hands can only
be described as false if one is using the term in a moral sense,
meaning hypocritical or insincere.

Not all representational art is realist. *The Divine Comedy*,
for example, or *The Cat in the Hat*. Works like this portray
people, places and events, but not of the kind we might come
across on Camden High Street. Dreams, fantasies and halluci-
nations can be just as representational as novels about drug
pushers on council estates. They are also in some sense real.
So are psychotic delusions, visions of eternal damnation or
nightmares of Tom Cruise appearing at one's bedside with a
maniacal grin. Nightmares about Tom Cruise are real in the
sense that one can really have them, but not in the sense that
he is actually perched on the end of one's bed. Mickey Mouse
is real in the sense that he is the product of certain material
technologies, but not in the sense that Calamity Jane was.
(There are, however, some apparently sane theorists of fiction
who believe that Sherlock Holmes is real, and that he actually
does play the violin. They also believe that the star ship *Enterprise* really does have a heat shield.)

There are realistic types of fantasy, meaning ones that might
in principle happen in real life (imagining that you are in

bed with a mongoose, for example, which is unlikely but not impossible), as well as unrealistic ones (imagining you are in bed with Queen Victoria). There are also literary works which present bizarre flights of fancy in a flat, everyday idiom. Franz Kafka writes a sober, economical prose, unruffled by the improbable events it records. Should we call such art realist, or is this to stretch the term beyond all usefulness? What of the fiction of Dostoevsky, which depicts manic or psychopathic states of mind in familiar settings, or Bram Stoker's *Dracula*, which mingles Gothic fantasy with realist narrative?

A distinction may be helpful here. Some literary art is realist in form but not in content. A realism of the signifier can be coupled with a non-realism of the signified. To put the point more simply, you can use everyday language about situations which are blatantly unrealistic, as in *Gulliver's Travels* or *Animal Farm*. Or you can describe commonplace events in profusely poetic terms, in which case a non-realism of the signifier is coupled with a realism of the signified. James Joyce's *Ulysses* is a case in point. So is the fiction of Gustave Flaubert, in which there is an ironic disparity between the banal content of the novels and the fastidious style in which it is presented. It is as though Flaubert's elaborately self-conscious writing detaches itself aloofly from the sordid stuff it handles, refusing to be contaminated by its own tawdry narratives. There are also works of art like *The Tempest* which are non-realist in both language and content, as well as fictional texts like Ernest Hemingway's *A Farewell to Arms* which are realist in both senses. It is probably better to confine the term 'realism' to the kind of writing which is not only representational, but which portrays a world which lies within the bounds of possibility, at least for a specific time and place. In this sense, realism presents us not simply with what is the case, but with what could in principle be the case. It is possible, for example, that George Clooney is a North Korean spy. It is also possible that you might lock up your mad wife for years on an upper floor of your country mansion. It is not possible, however, to be leashed to the ground like Gulliver by a swarm of humanoid creatures who are only a few inches high, or for a wolf to try to fool you that he is your grandmother.

Broadly speaking, then, realism is a question of verisimilitude. As Northrop Frye remarks, 'When what is written is *like* what is known, we have an art of extended or implied simile.'[34] The problem is deciding what counts as this. Grossly improbable coincidences in fiction are deemed to be unrealistic, yet they happen from time to time in real life. There are also novels which blend realism with myth and folklore. One thinks of the magic realism of writers like Gabriel García Márquez, in which fable and fantasy sit cheek by jowl with recognisably realist features – a discord between everyday reality and the bizarre or preternatural which invests the narrative as a whole with a curiously dreamlike quality. 'Magic realism' is an intriguing term, since if realism seems to mirror the world, magic also relies on doublings, mimings and strange affinities. 'I don't want realism, I want magic!' cries Blanche Dubois in

Tennessee Williams's play *A Streetcar Named Desire*, but the two may be on more intimate terms than she supposes.

Realism and ideology

Realism appears to give the reader the genuine article, free of embellishment or subjective distortion, but there are critics for whom this can have some troubling consequences. Fiction of this kind may strike us as having the backing of reality itself, and may thus be invested with an authority which seems unimpeachable. This is especially true of omniscient narration, in which the reader has no choice but to accept the judgement of an anonymous narrator. It is also as though the voice of the narrator pulls rank over the speech of the characters themselves.[35] Realism sets up a pecking order in which the omniscient narrator always has the last word. But first-person narration may be equally authoritative. If a novel opens with the statement 'For a long time I would go to bed early', there are no grounds on which the reader can respond 'Bloody liar!' or 'Who are you trying to fool?' We have no choice but to accept the declaration, since there is nothing by which we might measure its truth or falsehood.

By contrast, some modernist art plays off one way of seeing against another, as with Cubism, montage, Surrealism or the theatre of Bertolt Brecht. Modernist works may also draw attention to their own limits, gesturing to truths which fall outside their frame of reference. They may intimate that there is more to reality than they themselves have captured. Poets and novelists may also thicken their language to highlight the fact that this is the stuff of art, rather than some incontestable reality which lies behind it. The language of realism, by contrast, may be so luminously transparent that we feel ourselves to be in the presence of reality itself, not of a specific way of illustrating it. We are expected to overlook the fact that what we are being offered is simply one possible version of the world. On this estimate, realism 'naturalises' what it presents, persuading us to treat it as self-evident. Since it may be in the interests of those who wield power for us to believe that, say, stock markets or gross inequalities are also here to stay, one can speak of such art as a form of ideology.

Ideology on this view presents itself as an 'Of course!' or 'It goes without saying'. It makes mass unemployment seem as inevitable as sunshine. A classic statement of the case can be found in the work of Roland Barthes, who regards myth or ideology as making things appear more innocent than they are. Myth, he writes, 'gives (things) a natural and eternal justification, it gives them a clarity which is not that of an explanation but of a statement of fact'.[36] 'The writing of Realism,' Barthes argues elsewhere, 'is far from being neutral; it is on the contrary loaded with the most spectacular signs of fabrication.'[37] Catherine Belsey, who shares this view, takes issue with what she calls 'classic realism' on several grounds. In her judgement, it is illusionistic, falsely transparent, blind to contradiction and convinced that truth (or 'truth', as postmodernists might coyly put it) is unproblematic. Writing of this kind, Belsey argues, is driven by a need for order and stability, shutting off a diversity of interpretations in its drive for closure. Since representations are largely static, realism is unable to present a fluid, self-contradictory world. All it can do is lend a spurious solidity to a reality that secretly resists it. Moreover, in striving for coherence, it helps to insulate the reader from conflict and ambiguity. It can confront us with struggle and contradiction, so its critics maintain, but only at the level of content. All this turmoil is contained by the unity of the form, which seeks to integrate the work into a harmonious whole. There is a good deal of antagonism and disorder in *Pride and Prejudice*, but the unifying narrative can take this in its stride.

Realism, it is claimed, creates a fictional world which reduces the unknown to the comfortably familiar. It is as though we cannot get enough of seeing our own reflection in the looking-glass. One effect of this may be to legitimate the status quo, as well as to reinforce the reader's sense of identity rather than unsettling it. In this view, then, we are dealing with a politically conservative form, whatever the occasionally radical nature of its content. There may be problems in reality, but reality is not problematic in itself, as it is for many a modernist writer. As Friedrich Nietzsche writes, 'Look, isn't our need for knowledge precisely this need for the familiar, the will to uncover under everything strange, unusual and questionable something that no longer disturbs us? Is it not the instinct of fear that bids us to know?'[38]

Realism helps to satisfy our idle, unquenchable curiosity about the world around us, rather as we may be mesmerised by a TV soap opera even though (or even because) we are aware that nothing of great moment is likely to happen. It is possible to watch people in the street from a cafe window with all the fascination of one who has never clapped eyes on a human creature before. In the end, what holds us captive about soap operas, over and above sheer inquisitiveness, is *happening itself* – our insatiable desire to watch events unfold before our eyes, as well as to find out what comes next. We might even be wary of sudden breaks or dramatic crises, since they threaten to undermine our assurance that the stuff of reality will continue to trundle on in the same old style. Curiosity is one of the chief reasons why we read realist fiction. It is a form of people-watching which saves us from having to leave our living room.

Catherine Belsey's charge sheet against the form is long enough for it to be put away for good if convicted. Yet a case can be made for the defence. Why, for example, should an appeal to the routine be conservative, and the act of disrupting it radical? Caring for disabled children is a routine enough task for some people. Coal-mining communities were a familiar fact of British life before a neoliberal government destroyed them. Conversely, the unknown – all-out nuclear warfare, Bangladesh sunk beneath the ocean – is not always an inviting prospect. And why is sabotaging the received wisdom always preferable to embracing it? What if the wisdom in question includes outlawing racial discrimination? Besides, are there not social groups whose identities need reinforcing rather than undermining? Do we admire works of art which do not only question their readers' identities as socialists or feminists but brutally subvert them?

It is true that some ideology 'naturalises' the cultural or historical, making it seem unchanging and inevitable. A classic example is the philosopher Thomas Hobbes's description of colonies as the 'children' of metropolitan nations, which makes Britain's acquisition of India sound as natural as having a baby.[39] Yet not all ideology works in this way. The Roman Catholic doctrine of the Virgin Mary's Immaculate Conception is ideological, but only its most seriously weird supporters would regard it as self-evident. A lot of people revere the monarchy, but not many devout royalists imagine that there has to be a monarch, and most of them are aware that there are societies without kings or queens which do not fall apart on this account. You can be committed to liberal democracy while being perfectly aware that it is of fairly recent origin, and that there are alternative ways of organising political life. Ideology can also be ironically conscious of itself, which would not be possible if it were simply taken-for-granted. 'Sorry to be such a slave to petty-bourgeois respectability, but would you mind actually wearing some clothes during the degree ceremony?' is an example. A true liberal must be liberal enough to be sceptical of his own liberalism. Like the novelist E.M. Forster, he must acknowledge the material privilege which allows him his tolerance and open-mindedness.

In any case, the naturalisation case seems to assume that Nature is immutable, which is far from true. Thomas Hardy's novel *The Return of the Native* opens with a well-known account of the supposedly changeless landscape of Egdon Heath, a tract of land that was planted from end to end by the Forestry Commission not long after the author's death. Hardy, whose vision of the world is nothing if not ironic, would surely have relished the fact. We shall be revisiting this gloomy location later on. It is enough for now to point out the strangeness of regarding Nature as static in an age when the stuff is continually being hacked around to suit our needs. It is far easier to move a mountain than to demolish patriarchy. In any case, one should beware of using the word 'natural' in a purely pejorative sense, as most postmodern thinkers do. It is natural to sleep, laugh, delight in the company of others or grieve over the death of a loved one. It is also worth noting that the aversion to Nature in some recent theory is not unrelated to its gradual elimination in practice. In both cases, culture exerts supreme dominion over the natural world. Postmodernism doesn't much care for Nature, and neither does the mining industry.

Nature can be a radical, even revolutionary idea. Like the concept of reason, it was wielded by some eighteenth-century Enlightenment thinkers as a weapon against rank, privilege and inequality. One of the most astonishingly best-selling political tracts ever published, Thomas Paine's *The Rights of Man*, uses the concept in precisely this sense. There is no class-distinction or cultural supremacy in Nature, a fact which can be turned against the artifice of social divisions. What we share in common with others of our species is, or ought to be, more fundamental than accidents of birth or upbringing. The idea of difference is not always on the side of the political angels. Nobody celebrates the difference between a slave and his master, apart perhaps from the master. In our own time, it is not so much Nature as the defence of it from a predatory humanity which has become a form of radical politics.

The complaint that realism rebuffs alternative ways of seeing is equally suspect. Is a piece of feminist fiction to be rebuked because it fails to promote a patriarchal view of the world as well? Where do you draw the line between pluralism and spineless liberalism? Is all closure to be demonised? The truth of statements like 'Sex trafficking should not be condoned', or 'There were Nazis who regarded Jews as subhuman', should not be treated as purely provisional. As for unity and stability, a reasonable degree of these things is essential for human well-being. Unity need not be monolithic, and stability is not synonymous with stagnation. All human beings need some sense of orientation, which need not rule out being open to the new and unsettling. Postmodern critics may be sceptical of the settled and rooted, but migrants who have risked their necks to get to Europe are unlikely to be of this opinion. Besides, the problem with late capitalist society is that there is too little order and stability, not too much – that in the constant agitation of the marketplace it is impossible to snatch a few moments of sleep.

Perhaps readers of realist fiction are not always as gullible as this mildly patronising case makes out. Realism strikes a tacit contract with its audience, by which they agree to suspend their disbelief in its claims. Instead, they grant a provisional assent to what it portrays. This is a different matter from believing that Hobbits actually scuttle across one's garden at twilight. Samuel Johnson remarked that while watching a play an audience never ceases to be conscious that it is in a theatre, and much the same applies to reading realist literature. Anyway, even if a novel takes for granted an indefensible view of humanity, it is always open to the reader to reject it. The views of non-realist works may be just as objectionable. There are also plenty of realist novels, from Stendhal and Balzac to Dickens, Hardy, Zola and Gissing, which challenge received versions of reality rather than tamely transmit them. Are radical critiques of Victorian England such as *Little Dorrit* and *Tess of the d'Urbervilles* to be censured on account of their realist form? Was everything from Defoe to Dostoevsky a ghastly mistake?

Despite praising realism as 'one of the most complex and vital realisations of Western culture',[40] Fredric Jameson speaks a little long-windedly of the 'structural and inherent conservatism and anti-politicality of the realist novel as such', insisting that

> an ontological realism, absolutely committed to the density and solidity of what is – whether in the realm of psychology and feelings, institutions, objects or space – cannot but be threatened in the very nature of the form

by any suggestion that these things are changeable and not ontologically immutable: the very choice of the form itself is a professional endorsement of the status quo, a loyalty oath in the very apprenticeship to this aesthetic.

Realism, he remarks, 'has a vested interest, an ontological stake, in the solidity of social reality, on [sic] the resistance of bourgeois society to history and social change'.[41] A realist novel may clamour for social change; but (so the theory goes) the sheer sturdiness of the world it presents, its stolid air of being here to stay, threatens to undercut this demand. The form, in a word, is in contradiction with the content.

The claim, however, is surely overstated. For one thing, a resistance to revolutionary change need not mean a resistance to change as such. On the contrary, realism and mutability are closely linked. In his study of Paul Cézanne, *If These Apples Should Fall*, the art historian T.J. Clark writes that to be true to life, a painting must be full of the sense of how things could have been otherwise. Nor is it true that middle-class society is hostile to history. On the contrary, as Marx points out in *The Communist Manifesto*, dynamism, upheaval and ceaseless innovation are its watchwords. Jameson is mistaken to think that realism is in love with the static and perpetual. The critic John Brenkman dismisses as a caricature the idea that nineteenth-century realism mirrors a stable reality.[42] Besides, there is nothing radical about change itself, and what stays the same is not always to be spurned. If the Kremlin and

Pentagon have a permanent look about them, so does the demand for racial justice. Mutability is not always to be affirmed, and not all social change is to be celebrated. It is to be hoped that there will be no return to child labour or the hanging of petty thieves.

If realism, as Jameson argues, is nervous of upheaval, what of the Jacobin and Chartist novel, along with feminist, utopian and working-class fiction? One might add to this list a lineage of radical realist drama, from Henrik Ibsen to Sarah Kane. It is true that realist fiction is not generally at its finest when it deals with the sphere of day-to-day politics. The fiction of Trollope or Disraeli, which does just this, scarcely outshines the writings of Melville and Turgenev. Yet there is a sense in which this is to the credit of the realist novel, not a fault to be regretted. Authors like Balzac, Scott, Eliot and Tolstoy delve deeper than the cut and thrust of the political domain to explore the fundamental social forces which shape it. In this sense, the classical realist novel, with its diverse, densely populated landscapes, its ability to shift from one area of activity to another and lay bare their hidden affiliations, is a richer literary form than tales of party-political intrigue. The same is true of the way it can register certain stealthy historical developments buried deep beneath the surface of everyday life.

All of which is to say that if realism is inherently conservative (a claim which we have taken leave to doubt), it may sometimes be so in a positive sense. Refusing to confine its attention to a political elite, it seeks in democratic spirit to chart a far broader span of social life. It can, so to speak, hand the microphone to any of its characters, however inconspicuous. It has an implicit conviction that political changes and convulsions must be anchored in the sentiments of the common people, which is one reason why realist fiction tends to be sceptical of clean breaks or quick political fixes. Politics must respect the complexity of the common life – a complexity figured in George Eliot's *Middlemarch* as a web of interwoven strands. The social is more fundamental than the political, which is (or should be) in the service of its needs.

Franco Moretti is another who insists that realist fiction, anxious to preserve the coherence and continuity of its narratives, 'chooses to pass over revolutionary fractures in silence'. Instead, its material is the stuff of everyday life, which requires

an unchallenged stability of social relationships. But if this stability comes undone, and history starts to run, farewell everyday life – farewell 'personality', 'conversation', 'episode', 'experience', 'harmony'. It is once again the incompatibility between the novelistic world and revolutionary crisis . . . revolutionary crisis undermines everyday life.[43]

But it is not obvious that this is so. During the Dublin uprising against British colonial rule in 1916, the *Irish Times* went on being published and the Shelbourne, the finest hotel in town, continued to serve high tea. All revolutions leave more things unchanged than transformed. People still need bread or even babysitters in the midst of political unrest. What changes them fundamentally are not political insurrections but the long social and cultural revolutions which may follow in their wake. In any case, there are plenty of novels which feature militant insurgencies of one kind or another. William Morris's utopian *News from Nowhere* provides the reader with a strikingly convincing account of how a socialist revolution might come about in Britain. It is not so much realism that is hostile to revolutionary ruptures as the middle-class civilisation that produces it. There seems little in the form itself, as opposed to the views of some of its practitioners, to warrant dismissing it as politically benighted.

3

WHAT IS REALISM? (2)

Realism, art and illusion

For some critics of realism, works of art which draw attention to their own artifice are inherently subversive, since they refuse to pass themselves off as the undeniable truth. This is surely untrue. The phrase 'Once upon a time' has come to signify 'This is a story', and thus to warn us not to take what follows as fact; but this fails to turn 'Snow White and the Seven Dwarfs' into an insurrectionary tract, unless the dwarfs are to be regarded as an oppressed underclass. There are, to be sure, authors who are anti-realist in their art and radical in their politics (Bertolt Brecht, Virginia Woolf), but there are others like Ezra Pound, Jorge Luis Borges and Vladimir Nabokov who are anti-realist in art yet politically conservative. Nor is it true that all realist writing is deceptively transparent. Realism, too, can draw attention to its forms and techniques from time to time. It is not always blind to what it is about.

All such critiques of the form, remarks Matthew Beaumont, regard it as

> an exercise in illusionism that is at once naive and intellectually dishonest. It implies that all realism is a species of *trompe l'oeil*, an act of representation that, in replicating external reality as scrupulously as possible, dreams of attaining an exact correspondence to it. It is a conception of realism that at the same time overstates its mimetic ambitions and dramatically undervalues its ability to exhibit and examine the formal limitations that shape it.[1]

The case, in a word, is a caricature. It is true, as we have seen, that a lot of realist art is poorer in formal conventions than most other literary modes, which is part of the price it must sometimes pay for its candour. It may need to sacrifice style to substance. Yet not all such art purports to offer us a flawless window on to the truth. Realist fiction can reflect in critical or ironic spirit on how it stages reality. It can seem to despair of ever capturing the truth of a character or condition, or gesture to the possibility of alternative worlds. The novels of Anthony Trollope are standard realist works which seek to pass themselves off as slices of real life, yet Henry James complains that Trollope 'took a suicidal satisfaction in reminding the reader that the story he was telling was only, after all, a make-believe'.[2] Even for the reader to exclaim 'How lifelike!' is for her to confess that what she has in her hands is an artful contrivance. You would not say this of a bus ticket.

In any case, those who rebuke realist art for its deceptive clarity should beware of belittling the value of transparency. They neglect realism's power to dispel the obscurantism which shrouds certain political set-ups, of which the fog in Dickens's *Bleak House* is a memorable symbol. When Blake rails against the occult rituals of priest and king, he does so in the name of a lucidity which, pressed to its limit, is so intense as to be well-nigh unbearable. It is this luminosity that is meant by the mystical – a state of mind which is the enemy of mystification rather than its accomplice. Traditionally, the mystical involves a vision of the Real (for which one name is God) so intense and overpowering as to beggar speech and stretch the imagination to infinity. In aesthetic terms, it is known as the sublime.

Editing one's narrative is indispensable to literary realism, but it can also be problematic. Realist fiction may seem to give the reader a blow-by-blow account of reality, but what it offers us is artfully shaped and selected. For the reader to be too conscious of this, however, threatens to unmask the realist illusion. Art must be designed, yet how then can it be true to the disorderly nature of reality? 'The realistic writer,' observes Northrop Frye, 'soon finds that the requirements of literary form and plausible content always fight against each other.'[3] To ensure a happy ending, for example, you need to grant the virtuous characters their just desserts and the villains their comeuppance, neither of which might happen if this were a true history. Many a fictional hero who ends up with a comely wife and a sizeable landed estate would probably have been hanged in real life. Since these rewards are unlikely to occur spontaneously, the novel itself may have to step in and engineer them. And since this is hard to pull off without a degree of manipulation, the story risks generating just the air of unreality it hopes to avoid. The gap between actual and poetic justice looms embarrassingly large. Jane Eyre is able to marry Rochester, but only because the novel steps in and kills off his first wife. Verisimilitude is sacrificed to our utopian longing for happiness.

Not all writers feel content with this form of closure, not least modernist ones. 'Some people – and I am one of them – hate happy ends', reflects Vladimir Nabokov in his novel *Pnin*. 'We feel cheated. Harm is the norm. Doom should not jam. The avalanche stopping in its tracks a few feet from the cowering village behaves not only unnaturally but unethically.' What Nabokov objects to is not so much resolutions as cheerful ones. Realism should be bleak, since that is the way the world is. There is something synthetic about happiness. That real life is a sombre, squalid affair is a typically modern assumption. It is worth speculating on how this opinion arises. Perhaps it is a consequence of industrial blight, or the fact that the twentieth century was by far the bloodiest on record. Yet beauty and elegance can be quite as real as their opposites. In fact, some scientists regard them as a sign that their hypotheses are trustworthy. Not all harmony or symmetry is to be dismissed as anodyne.

An author might believe, or feign to believe, that editing his material is a way of cheating on the reader, and is thus morally unacceptable. Design is deceit. Art and integrity are mutually at odds. Surely your audience deserves the whole truth, without being short-changed by gaps and silences? To recount your life history, for example, you may need to provide the reader with an exhaustive account of your everyday experience from birth onwards, leaving nothing out. In the great web of human affairs, who knows what apparently trifling incident might have had a momentous effect on your development? Perhaps it is important for this purpose to push your narrative back beyond birth to your time in the womb, or even further back to the moment of conception.

To present one's readers with this sprawling mass of information, however, is to risk disorientating them altogether, as one digression opens on to another and the narrator finds himself unable to say one thing without pursuing half a dozen others. The text begins to proliferate beyond its author's control. The more laboriously he stitches it together, the more it threatens to fall apart. It is not long before we start to suspect that his good-humoured solicitude towards his readers, his efforts to keep them alert and informed, is really a thinly disguised form of sadism. Under cover of total honesty, we are being taken for one of the longest rides in literary history. Since the narrator continues to live in the present while writing about his past, he would need to put his life on hold in order to catch up with himself. The more he writes, the more he will have to write, since the more living he will have got through in the meanwhile. And if his life history is to be complete, he would need to include the act of writing it in his account of it.

Such is the hilariously eccentric world of Laurence Sterne's eighteenth-century anti-novel, *Tristram Shandy*, the protagonist of which has still not got himself born by the end of the first two volumes of his autobiography. Walter Shandy, Tristram's insanely rationalist father, seeks to impose some order on this hotchpotch of misadventures, but like a third-rate novelist finds his shapely schemes buried beneath a rising tide of pure contingency. Almost before the realist novel has got off the ground in England, Sterne, a semi-outsider who hailed from Tipperary, has spotted the sheer impossibility of the realist project in any literal sense of the term, and proceeds to reap comic fiction from the fact.

Sterne's art may be gloriously muddled, but as an Anglican cleric he presumably believed that history was not. Instead, it was a story of fall and redemption. Generally speaking, people in modern times have ceased to believe that history itself is story-shaped – that it represents a tale of progress or Providence, or that there is some grand narrative afoot of which our own humble lives form a minor part. One can find a muted form of this belief as late as George Eliot, but it is dead on its feet by the time we arrive at Thomas Hardy. If the world has an objective structure to it, then a realist work of art can reproduce reality in all its intricate detail while preserving a certain shapeliness. Once things come to seem purely haphazard, however, you may need to foist an arbitrary design on them; yet the more disorderly they are, the more elaborate your design may have to be, growing too conspicuous and thereby endangering the truth-effect of your art.

There are those who argue that to ditch verisimilitude, as many modernist works do, is more realist than realism itself. Isn't it more truthful to see the world as fragmentary and conflictive rather than to place one's faith in some providential order, which scarcely sounds like a realistic proposition to anyone who has been reading the newspapers? Perhaps the ultimate realism is to acknowledge that artistic realism itself is a cunning illusion. Fredric Jameson speaks of

> the simultaneous assertion that realism is the most complex epistemological instrument yet devised for recording the truth of social reality, and at one and the same time, that it is a lie in the very form itself, the prototype of aesthetic false consciousness, the appearance that bourgeois ideology takes on in the realm of narrative literature.[4]

Most literary theorists, as it happens, would not regard realist fiction as a lie, though neither of course would they take it to be true. Lies are designed to deceive, whereas *Lord of the Flies* is not. Nobody is really asking us to believe that Captain Ahab died leashed to a whale called Moby-Dick. It has also been claimed that propositions in fiction are neither true nor false because they are not really propositions at all. They simply have the grammatical appearance of them. As we have seen, they are present to pull their weight in a fictional world, not as scraps of real-life information. Even if a piece of fiction is factually accurate down to the last detail, the fact that we call it fiction in the first place means that its factual truth or falsehood is irrelevant. Taking a real-life report without altering a word and calling it a novel or short story changes the relationship of the reader to the text. Among other things, it invites the reader to look for some general moral truth in the work, rather than taking it simply as a specific account with no deeper implications.

So Jane Austen does not expect us to believe that Emma Woodhouse was handsome, clever and rich. Nor, however, is it true that she was ugly, dim-witted and on her uppers, since no such person ever existed. Even if there had been a handsome, clever and rich woman called Emma Woodhouse at the time the work was written, one, moreover, who resembled Austen's heroine in every respect, the novel would not be about her. The very act of calling it a novel rules this out. In Wallace Stevens's poem 'The Idea of Order at Key West' there is a passing reference to Ramon Fernandez, who was a well-known literary critic at the time, and who is described as being pale. We know that Stevens was aware of Fernandez's existence, indeed had read some of his work. Fernandez may not have been pale in real life, or Stevens may not have known whether he was or not; but for poetic reasons he is pale in the work, which is all that matters. And 'poetic' here means more than just the sound and cadence of his name; it also includes the part it plays in the poem's moral vision.

The realist novel breaks with a range of older literary modes: epic, allegory, romance, legend, fairy tale, folk tale, moral fable and the like. As Harry Levin observes, it has assimilated many other forms over the centuries: 'essays and letters, memoirs and chronicles, dialogues and rhapsodies, religious tracts and revolutionary manifestoes, sketches of travel and books of etiquette, every kind of prose and some kinds of verse'.[5] It is the most omnivorous genre in history, absorbing almost everything in print it finds ready to hand. The eighteenth-century novelist Henry Fielding describes his masterpiece *Tom Jones* as 'a comic epic in prose', juggling with traditional literary categories in order to classify a kind of writing for which there is as yet no established name. 'History' is the eighteenth century's nearest approximation to what will later be known as the novel.

Yet the novel's break with previous writing, at least until recent times, has rarely been complete. A good deal of realism is parasitic on previous literary forms, rather as a lot of modernist art continues to depend on the very realism it spurns. To be effective, experiments with reality must rely on some sense of how things usually function. Deviations imply the existence of norms. Franz Kafka's *Metamorphosis*, in which the protagonist wakes up one morning to find himself turned into a giant insect, would not work unless we were familiar with the fact that people do not generally turn into beetles over-night. People to whom this happens with tedious regularity might treat the fable as realist. All art, however freakish or fantastic, has a relation to reality, in the sense that we could make nothing of a phenomenon which lay entirely beyond the frontiers of our experience. As long as aliens from Alpha Centauri travel about the cosmos in space craft, speak to those they abduct in robotic voices and take a clinical interest in their genitals, they are really not aliens at all, regardless of whether they stink of sulphur and have no idea who Britney Spears is.

Fredric Jameson writes of how the novel form 'desacralises' social reality. It punctures the illusions of fable and romance and strips the halo of holiness from the world. In pre-modern societies, Jameson argues, things are invested with symbolic, mythological or supernatural meaning. For middle-class civilisation, by contrast, they are simply, starkly themselves.[6] With the emergence of realism, we are speaking of a 'desacralised, post-magical, commonsense, everyday, secular reality'.[7] The realist novel is a form appropriate to what the sociologist Max Weber calls a disenchanted world. Yet myth, fable, magic and the supernatural do not simply vanish. When realism encounters problems which cannot be tackled in its own terms, it may turn to the resources of magic and fairy tale to pull off an unlikely resolution. The discovery of a long-lost relative with money to burn and an avuncular affection for the penniless heroine; the revelation that you are not brother and sister after all and so are free to marry; the messenger appearing on horseback waving a royal pardon as the noose begins to tighten around the hero's neck: all these devices suggest how realist fiction continues to be indebted to the non-realist art it has supposedly superannuated. It is only when such fiction abandons the need for closure – as, strikingly, with the novels of D.H. Lawrence – that it can discard these contrivances.

Realism and Thomas Hardy

You may also draw on myth, symbolism and the supernatural to dignify what might otherwise be dismissed as inconsequential. Such is the case with Thomas Hardy's *The Return of the Native*, which like most of Hardy's novels has a realist setting in the English West Country, but which is determined that this provincial spot should not be allowed to diminish the genuine human tragedies which unfold there. This is why the story starts with a rather grand, self-conscious set piece describing the Heath itself, in which the author is on his best literary behaviour:

> The sombre stretch of rounds and hollows seemed to rise and meet the evening gloom in pure sympathy, the heath exhaling darkness as rapidly as the heavens precipitated it. And so the obscurity in the air and the obscurity in the land closed together in a black fraternisation towards which each advanced half-way . . . It was at present a place perfectly accordant with man's nature – neither ghastly,

hateful, nor ugly: neither commonplace, unmeaning, nor tame; but, like man, slighted and enduring; and withal singularly colossal and mysterious in its swarthy monotony. As with some persons who have long lived apart, solitude seemed to look out of its countenance. It had a lonely face, suggesting tragical possibilities.

This, one can imagine Hardy thinking, is the kind of thing which should go down well in the metropolis, which likes its fiction to be 'literary'. It might also do no harm for such civilised readers to know that a country bumpkin is able to churn this stuff out. Quite a few of his readers saw him as a purveyor of charming bucolic tales who sometimes grew a little too big for his literary boots. Laboriously overwritten phrases like 'singularly colossal and mysterious in its swarthy monotony' suggest that the author is trying rather too hard. In the novel as a whole, however, he allows this highly-wrought 'poetical' account of the Heath to lie cheek by jowl with a more realist view of it, as a workaday place in which the book's characters live and labour. If the Heath is a brooding symbolic presence, it is also a source of livelihood, and Hardy has a curious tolerance for this kind of incongruity.

There are times when the novel wheels up some rather creaky mythological imagery in order to invest its 'low life' materials with a grander, more 'literary' air. Eustacia Vye, a young countrywoman whose chief ambition in life, apart from being loved to madness, is to live in the fashionable seaside resort of Budmouth (Bournemouth), is presented as a 'Queen of the Night', 'the raw material of a divinity'. Hardy writes:

> She had Pagan eyes, full of nocturnal mysteries . . . Her presence brought memories of such things as Bourbon roses, rubies, and tropical midnights; her moods recalled lotus-eaters and the march in 'Athalie'; her motions, the ebb and flow of the sea; her voice, the viola. In a dim light, and with a slight rearrangement of her hair, her general figure might have stood for that of either of the higher female deities.

This off-the-peg exoticism is so blatantly non-realist that it is hard not to see it as ironic. Or perhaps it floats ambiguously between irony and a sincere attempt at so-called fine writing. Or maybe Hardy didn't know which it was himself. If it isn't ironic, then it springs from the author having his eye on the writing rather than the character. It is difficult to credit that this passage is speaking of the daughter of a Bournemouth bandmaster, and almost impossible to believe that it is not aware of this bathos. The same discrepancy is true in a more minor key of the book's male protagonist, Clym Yeobright, a reputable middle-class figure who ends up as an archetypal Scholar Gypsy or itinerant preacher. The two dimensions of the narrative, realist and anti-realist, converge quite literally in the person of Diggory Venn, a dealer in the red ochre with which farmers mark their sheep. Covered in red dye from head to foot by virtue of his trade, Venn hovers between being a run-of-the-mill rural workman and a spooky, mythological figure who Hardy originally intended to disappear mysteriously from the tale.

As the son of a small-time Dorset builder, Hardy was well aware that the English countryside of the time 'suggested tragical possibilities' in a rather more prosaic sense than his description of the Heath could accommodate. It was a place struggling with poverty, unemployment, falling profits, cut-throat foreign competition, trade union militancy, the loss or decline of traditional skills and customs and a steady haemorrhage of the population to the industrial cities. The title of the chapter describing the Heath is 'A Face on which Time Makes but Little Impression', which, as Hardy was well aware, was certainly not true of the English countryside in general in the late nineteenth century.

Despite this, Hardy's fiction occasionally reaches back beyond realism to the pastoral tradition. In *Far from the Madding Crowd*, he writes of a barn and the country people who use it as being 'natural' to each other, even though the same bunch of labourers are also shown to be so inept that they are incapable of extinguishing a fire. Nor does the novel disguise the fact that its hero, Gabriel Oak, can lose his employment as a small-time farmer almost overnight. The world of *The Mayor of Casterbridge* is one of uncertain harvests and unstable prices. This is not the image of rural life as tranquil, organic and picturesque beloved of English town-dwellers, for whom

Nature is a landscape to be contemplated rather than a place to work in. As Raymond Williams remarks, work figures more centrally in Hardy's writing than in any English novel of comparable importance.[8] Jane Austen, for example, looks at a piece of land and has a keen eye for its value and ownership, but she does not see anyone working there.

Hardy's novels do not deal with the English peasantry, a class which had been largely driven from the land by the time he came to write. What he presents instead is a capitalist, market-oriented economy based largely on landowners, tenant farmers and landless labourers. There is also a lower middle class of craftsmen, traders, dealers, teachers, artisans and others which is rapidly dwindling. It was this insecure social stratum which produced Hardy himself. Though sometimes patronisingly described as 'self-educated', meaning that he didn't attend either Oxford or Cambridge, he was trained as a professional architect. The protagonist of *The Mayor of Casterbridge*, Michael Henchard, is a grasping profiteer, while Tess Durbeyfield is no innocent child of Nature but a reasonably well-educated young woman who can speak Standard English when she chooses to do so. Jude Fawley of *Jude the Obscure* is not a peasant but a skilled artisan. Despite its idyllic title, one craftily designed for metropolitan consumption, *Under the Greenwood Tree* is much concerned with social snobbery and sexual competition. There are times when *The Woodlanders* exudes a sense of harmony and fertility, but it is a curiously self-conscious, almost self-parodying version of pastoral.

Because of his ambiguous position as a writer, portraying a rural England in which he was reared with one canny eye on a metropolitan readership, Hardy has a problem about what kind of fiction to write. If he belongs to the agrarian world he describes, he is also a semi-outsider in this community by virtue of his education and status as an author. His voice is sometimes that of the knowledgeable countryman, sometimes that of the detached observer. It is just these conflicts which make his fiction so intriguing. He has at his disposal a wide range of literary forms – realism, romance, pastoral, folk tale, high tragedy, psychological drama – and tends to shift from one to the other without feeling any pressing need to paper over the cracks. As with Eustacia Vye and Diggory Venn, two incompatible ways of seeing may be overlaid on each other, one realist and the other not.

Hardy's realism is 'impure' because it looks back to more traditional literary forms, but also because it strives towards a still indescribable future. This is most evident in his last novel *Jude the Obscure*, which caused such outrage that Hardy declared himself cured of all further desire to write. With its assault on marriage, the church, orthodox sexual mores and a higher educational system closed to working people, *Jude* has something of the scandalous quality of French naturalism without its clinical ethos. It undermines Victorian expectations not least by a melancholic ending, in which the protagonist dies in despair while reciting from the Book of Job. To appreciate the audacity of this, one needs to imagine

Oliver Twist falling downstairs and breaking his neck on the novel's last page. One of the roles of fiction, some Victorians maintained, was to edify and uplift, since gloom was regarded as ideologically dangerous. Disaffection breeds dissent. Once it infects the working classes, it can bear fruit in the form of insurrection. The same was considered true of atheism, even by middle-class commentators who no more believed in God themselves than they did in leprechauns. Hardy and George Eliot are the first major, self-avowedly godless novelists of English literature.

One might contrast the first paragraph of *The Return of the Native* with the spare, uncivil opening of *Jude the Obscure*: 'The schoolmaster was leaving the village, and everybody seemed sorry. The miller at Cresscombe lent him the small white tilted cart and horse to carry his goods to the city of his destination, about twenty miles off'. It seems a suitably ungarnished beginning for what is to prove an abrasively realist work. Yet the book is also crammed with episodes which boldly defy realist expectations. Its heroine, Sue Bridehead, leaps out of the bedroom window to avoid the sexual attentions of her middle-aged husband. A more forward woman angles for Jude's attention by throwing a pig's penis at him. Jude drunkenly recites the Nicene Creed in an Oxford pub, while his and Sue's adopted son hangs their two other children and then inflicts the same catastrophe on himself. All this, along with Jude and Sue's unmarried status as sexual partners, is a calculated affront to late Victorian England. It is no wonder that the Bishop of Wakefield, disgusted with the novel's 'insolence and indecency', threw it into the fire. The book did, however, earn itself one or two backhanded compliments. None but a writer of exceptional talent, one reviewer lamented, could have produced so gruesome and despondent a work.

Sue Bridehead is one of the so-called New Women of the period, who has enlightened views about marriage and sexuality and is fighting for her own emancipation. Sexuality, she recognises, is largely about subjugation. As Hardy writes in *Far from the Madding Crowd*, 'it is difficult for a woman to express her feelings in a language which is chiefly made by men to express theirs'. *Jude the Obscure* sees with extraordinary insight that the sexual institutions of late Victorian society have destroyed the possibility of friendship between men and women. Yet feminism is only just emerging, and Sue's impulse to be free is at war with her guilt, self-loathing and yearning to submit. Hardy sympathises deeply with his heroine, but it is as though he cannot quite understand his own creation. There is a volatile, elusive, self-contradictory quality about this woman which makes it hard for the novel to get her into focus. To do so would mean breaking beyond the bounds of realism and speaking a different language altogether, one which was not primarily the creation of men. We are awaiting the arrival of Virginia Woolf. The same problem will confront D.H. Lawrence, who in *Sons and Lovers* touches on emotional intensities which the realist frame of the novel prevents him from fully exploring. In *The Rainbow*, a history of everyday life continually delves into an inward dimension which lies beyond the reach of realism. Then, in the audacious formal experiment of *Women in Love*, realist credibility is swept aside for a montage of symbolic episodes which flouts the very idea of what a novel is meant to be.

Necessity and contingency

'In the highest realism,' writes Raymond Williams, 'society is seen in fundamentally personal terms, and persons, through relationships, in fundamentally social terms.'[9] You cannot represent an abstraction called the economy, the class system or moral law. Instead, you must show these things in terms of closely observed situations peopled by convincingly drawn characters. This, like drawing on myth and fairy tale, can always help the realist writer out of a tight spot. Social problems can be converted into personal terms, which may make them rather more tractable. An example is Elizabeth Gaskell's novel *North and South*, which concerns the ferocious industrial class struggles of the 1840s. A hard-headed factory owner is confronted by a bunch of mutinous workers, but the woman he loves proves to be a soothing influence on his pride and the clash of interests is defused. Love is the way to quell class warfare, in fiction if not in real life. In fact, marriage in realist fiction is often a displaced version of social harmony. If it is a matter of mutual affection, it is also a question of rank and property. In this sense, it can serve to reconcile individual desire with social convention. Trying to square these two aspects of marriage is largely what Jane Austen's novels are about. In Romantic fiction, by contrast, desire and social convention are frequently at odds. One thinks again of *Jane Eyre*, in which the heroine's love for Rochester risks driving her beyond the bounds of polite society.

Realism seeks to square contingency with necessity. Real life is full of random events, whereas if a telephone keeps ringing in a piece of realist fiction, we would be bemused if it turned out to be simply a telephone ringing, with no bearing on the plot. We also know that many of the details to be found in a realist novel are arbitrarily selected, and as such may have no special meaning in themselves. The moustache described as bushy and tobacco-stained might just as well have been clipped and greying. Even so, such small touches, like a painter's delicate daubs, contribute to the overall air of reality. They are, as Roland Barthes remarks, significant in their insignificance.[10] They signify rather than denote, meaning that what is at stake is not the colour of a character's moustache but the subliminal message: 'This is realism.' Realism typically supplies us with a redundancy of information. Precisely because a detail isn't essential, the only reason for its presence would seem to be that it is true.

The New Testament is full of stray particulars which seem to testify to the truth of an event precisely because they are bathetic, off-beat or superfluous. We are told, for example, that the first of Jesus's followers to discover that he was no longer in his tomb were women – a claim which might well have proved an embarrassment to the Gospel writers, since women were not seen as credible witnesses at the time. In fact, their testimony was regarded as worthless. The incident may have been recorded simply because it was generally known, and so could not plausibly be left out. Mary Magdalene mistakes the risen Jesus for the cemetery gardener, while Peter, in the act of denying that he is a disciple of Jesus after his master's arrest, gives himself away by his Galilean accent. He later tells a crowd of onlookers that he and his comrades are speaking in tongues rather than drunk, since it is too early in the day for them to have downed much wine. Jesus tries to restore the sight of a blind man, but the man's vision remains blurred and Jesus has to try again, this time successfully. When he is about to raise Lazarus from the dead, Lazarus's sister Martha warns him that he has been in his tomb for some days and is likely to stink. When Jesus restores Jairus's daughter to life, he advises those around him to give her something to eat. He asks for something to eat himself when he appears to his disciples after his death, and they give him a piece of broiled fish. A young man listening to Paul's interminable preaching falls asleep beside an open window and topples out of it. These are examples of what Roland Barthes in *Camera Lucida* calls a 'punctum', meaning the kind of quirky detail which contributes to the 'reality effect' of a work.

In realist writing, however, chance is continually turning into necessity. What starts off as accidental may end up as ineluctable. Realist works may set up situations at will but then find themselves bound by their constraints. If the hero is co-matose at one point in a realist narrative he cannot be winning the Boston marathon ten seconds later, as could easily happen in a modernist work. There is a constant interplay in such writing between the contingent and the essential. A good deal of non-realism, by contrast, strips the text of all sense of neces-sity and allows contingency free play. The fiction of Samuel Beckett, in which everything seems makeshift and fortuitous, is a case in point. Beckett's work strips the mask from necessity, even if (like all fiction) it is constrained by an internal logic. In this respect, it issues an implicit rebuke to the vision of a divinely ordered universe. In doing so, however, it sails perilously close to the very theology it rejects. The Christian doctrine of Creation concerns the gratuitous nature of things, not their inevitability. It is about the fact that there is no need for anything at all, least of all human beings. Instead of something, there might just as well have been nothing. It is a Beckettian kind of reflection.

4

THE POLITICS OF REALISM

Realism and nominalism

For medieval Europe, realism was a philosophical rather than artistic concept. It consisted of the belief that general concepts like 'liver' or 'leopard' denoted something real, rather than just being names for a set of things which look alike. The latter view was promoted by the opponents of the realists, who were known as nominalists.[1] In their opinion, general concepts were simply names, with no reality to correspond to them. Realists claim that the world is made up of certain categories of things, and that these categories are somehow built into it. Nominalists, by contrast, argue that the world is a set of irreducibly particular items, which we ourselves group together in certain ways to suit our purposes. Is there a sense in which leopardness exists in reality, or is it simply an abstraction from a host of individual creatures? Are common natures real or are they fictional? Behind this disagreement lies an important question: does the world tell us how we are to carve it up conceptually, or is it purely up to us? If there are given natures, the answer would seem to be the former; if there are only particulars, it looks more like the latter.

If common natures are real, then this may set limits to what you can do with them. It may follow that things can put up some resistance to your designs on them. If, however, things have no given nature, they become more pliable, and so can be more easily pressed into your service. They can also be more easily manipulated. This applies among other things to human beings. Do they have certain intrinsic features simply by virtue of being human? Or are they wholly constituted by culture, and are thus more malleable? If there is such a thing as human nature, how come we can transform ourselves in the process we call history? Perhaps the answer is that human nature does not exclude the capacity for change. On the contrary, it may actually be built into it.

The running battle between realists and nominalists raises the question of how seriously one takes the specific qualities of things. For the realist camp, aspects of an object like its colour or texture are accidents, meaning that they are not essential to what it is. A brindled cow is as much a cow as a black-and-white one. For the nominalist camp, however, sensory particulars are strictly speaking all that exists. We can generalise from them to produce a concept, but such concepts are simply convenient fictions. They do not signify a nature which is real in the sense that Central Park is.

If things do have natures, so some realists argue, it is because they were endowed with them by God. God, to be sure, could always have made a different world from the one he has manufactured. He could have created birch trees that snore or roses that are ravaged by guilt, but he opted instead, however short-sightedly in retrospect, for the universe we see around us. To strip this world of its natures or essences, then, may involve stripping away divinity as well, since it is God who put these things there in the first place. In this sense, though plenty of nominalists were theologians, the theory springs from an increasingly secular world. It points the way from the premodern to the modern. Human investigation no longer feels constrained to respect the divinely created nature of things, which means that the project we know as science is free to blossom. We need scientific knowledge because divine wisdom did not determine the way the world is in advance. Knowledge can thus sever the cord that tethers it to theology. Humanity, no longer restrained by a sense of what is proper to its nature, is able to shake off its feudal and religious fetters to become the free, self-determining agent of modern times. There is a sharp exchange on this subject between Macbeth and Lady Macbeth. Since general concepts are increasingly out of favour, there is also a surge of interest in the specific. As Charles Taylor remarks, 'we can recognise with hindsight the nominalist "passion for the particular" as a major turning point in the history of Western civilisation'.[2] It is certainly one of the major sources of literary realism, as well as being central to Romanticism.

If human nature is a fiction, it may follow that human beings have nothing fundamentally in common. What is real above all is the individual, while social bonds have only a secondary reality. This belief plays a key role in the rise of possessive individualism.[3] Society is made up of a set of isolated individuals whose relations with each other are for the most part instrumental. Individual self-interest now reigns supreme. For the empiricist thought which accompanies this creed, the sensible is to be prized above the rational. The real is what you can smell, touch and taste, while theories and ideas are abstractions from this so-called sense data. The further from the concrete particular you move, the less real you get. Among other things, this may rule out theories of major social change. Radicals are fantasists lost in their bloodless abstractions, while conservatives are rooted in the palpable realities of family, region and religious faith.

Most modern literary types are natural-born nominalists. In fact, modern aesthetics was invented in mid eighteenth-century Germany as a so-called science of the concrete.[4] 'The movement away from theory and generality,' declares a character in Iris Murdoch's novel *Under the Net*, 'is the movement towards truth. All theorising is flight. We must be ruled by the situation itself and that itself is unutterably particular.' This surely can't be so. To identify a situation in the first place involves using concepts, and all concepts (including 'this', 'unique', 'inimitable', 'unutterably', 'particular' and so on) are inescapably general. Situations may be specific, but they are not 'unutterably' so. In some cases, not least those known as coincidences, their common features may be more striking than their differences. The philosopher Michael Polanyi writes that 'the belief that, since particulars are more tangible, their knowledge offers a true conception of things is fundamentally mistaken'.[5] In his view, it is not particulars which first seize our attention but patterns or unified wholes. In fact, it is the particular which is abstract, in the sense of being lifted from a larger context.

Having his philosophical cake and eating it, Aristotle maintains that general natures exist, but only in and through the specific. Samuel Johnson believed this too, along with other eighteenth-century neo-classical critics. Art must deal with general types, but in doing so it must particularise them. A landowner, for example, must be shown to behave in the way landowners typically do, but he must also be portrayed as *this* individual and not some other. Only in this way can art communicate universal truths while allowing us to feel these truths as tangibly as the smell of wood smoke. The specific in itself is too fleeting and trifling to claim our attention. What matters is the hero's moral character, not what he has for breakfast. An art of the ephemeral will not endure.[6] Essences are more important than accidents. One can contrast this view with that of some Romantic poets and theorists, for whom only *this* unique particular is capable of conveying *this* universal truth. The particular in question is known as a symbol.

The case of György Lukács

Samuel Johnson's insistence on the typical rather than accidental would have appealed to György Lukács, one of the most prominent apologists for literary realism of the modern age. He has been described as 'probably the greatest literary figure to have been produced by the Communist movement'.[7] In left-wing literary circles, he was certainly one of the most controversial. Literary critics these days are usually to be found in universities, but Lukács's turbulent career was conducted far from the college cloisters. He was a formidably erudite scholar of European culture who was also a professional revolutionary. Born in Budapest in 1885, he acted as deputy commissar for public education during the short-lived Hungarian Soviet Republic of 1919, and after the defeat of this experiment worked underground in his native country for a while. He spent several years in Vienna and Moscow, and in 1923 published his best-known work, *History and Class Consciousness*, which was denounced by a sizeable sector of the international Communist movement. When the Nazis came to power, Lukács fled to the Soviet Union. Despite being arrested and briefly gaoled on the charge of having been a Trotskyist agent, he managed to survive the ice age of Stalinism. After returning to Hungary, he supported an uprising against the nation's Soviet masters in 1956, and became minister of culture in a short-lived government. When the insurrection was violently suppressed he took flight once again.

Returning finally to his native Budapest, he died there in 1971. His career as insurrectionist, prisoner, political refugee and underground revolutionary makes for the kind of gripping realist narrative which he himself praised above all other artistic forms. His personal destiny was interwoven with a series of historic events in the manner of the realism he admired.

Much of Lukács's theory of literary realism derives from Hegel's writings on aesthetics. That he was so deeply indebted to an idealist philosopher did not sit well with some of his materialist colleagues, a fact which led him to recant this and other influences on a number of humiliating occasions. In works like *Studies in European Realism* and *The Historical Novel*, he sees realist fiction as revealing the fundamental currents and conflicts of society, yet at the same time unifying these conflicts into an artistic whole. Realism concerns itself with the typical, meaning the most significant historical developments from a Marxist viewpoint. But these must be given flesh and blood by the portrayal of credible individuals and events. Genuinely realist art combines typicality with individuality, which Lukács saw as a hallmark of Shakespeare and Balzac. So, indeed, did Karl Marx. By fusing the social and individual, this mode of art offers an alternative to the alienations of capitalist society, in which this unity is torn asunder. Lukács does not address an important criticism of this view, which is that by illustrating a general outlook with vividly concrete particulars, you may come to invest that outlook with all the solidity of the things that exemplify it, and so make it less disputable than it might otherwise be.

Realism, then, is not simply a question of technique. It is, so to speak, the way the world itself would wish to be represented, the art which reproduces its inmost structure. What Lukács calls critical realism, meaning the great tradition of the novel from Stendhal to Thomas Mann, is to his mind part of a precious heritage of middle-class humanism, one which needs to be reaffirmed in the face of a barbarous fascism. Modernism and fascism are seen as twin forms of irrationalism. Marxists should therefore not be afraid to rank bourgeois artists and thinkers as among their most revered ancestors. Marx himself, after all, learnt enduringly from Hegel, as well as from a number of prominent bourgeois economists.

In Lukács's view, there are latent historical forces working towards the achievement of socialism, though not in a deterministic way. It follows that literary works which dramatise these forces are progressive, whatever the political outlook of their authors. History itself is one-sided, so to speak, so that to portray it as it is is necessarily to be partisan. In fact, the author's political opinions are really neither here nor there. 'Tolstoy's case,' Lukács comments, 'is not the only case in the history of the world when a great artist creates immortal masterpieces on the basis of an entirely false philosophy.'[8] As backhanded compliments go, this one is hard to beat. As long as the historical conditions are ripe, literary works can seize upon the truth whatever the political standpoints of their authors. From Scott, Balzac and Stendhal to Tolstoy and Thomas Mann, the realists whom Lukács admires are by no means revolutionaries.

It is true that Lukács makes much of a writer's individual genius, in a move unusual for a Marxist. Yet historical conditions still take priority. Whether or not a work can capture the inner logic of history depends not just on the skill of the individual author, but on the historical moment to which he or she belongs. Realism is able to view that moment as a whole; and this is only possible when the class that produces it is still in a dynamic, forward-looking phase. Balzac is Lukács's prime example of this ability to grasp his situation as a totality. As middle-class society begins to degenerate, however, so critical realism starts to decline. For Lukács, the defeat of a series of popular insurrections in Europe in 1848 heralds the end of the 'progressive' phase of the bourgeoisie. As the capitalist order becomes too fragmented, opaque and conflict-ridden to be grasped as a total system, literary realism begins to wane.

The latest stage of this downturn is what Lukács sees as the calamity of modernism. The highpoint of the modernist movement coincides with the crack-up of middle-class civilisation known as the First World War – an era which witnesses not only military slaughter but social turmoil, economic crisis and political insurrection. Besieged by these troubles, the middle class loses whatever remains of its visionary power and proves incapable of further historical progress. What was once a revolutionary force wanes into a reactionary one. Its decline is hastened by the fact that a rival historical agent, the working-class movement, has now arrived on the scene. Only a social class which can grasp the overall logic of society is capable of revolutionary action; and this means that the working class must inherit the broad social vision which the middle class achieved in its heyday.

A good deal of modernist art turns its eyes from this ravaged historical landscape and beats a retreat into the autonomy of art. The concrete is sacrificed to the abstract. In the alienated worlds of Kafka, Proust, Musil, Joyce, Beckett, Camus and others, so Lukács argues, objective reality petrifies or falls to pieces. The world is now incoherent and impenetrable. It is no longer possible to grasp as a complex totality, in the manner of the great realist writers. Cynicism and nihilism set the artistic tone. 'Modernism,' Lukács complains, 'exalts bourgeois life's very baseness and emptiness with its aesthetic devices.'[9] Literature becomes morbidly obsessed with the aberrant and psychopathic. As human subjects are trapped in a social vacuum, they, too, begin to fall apart at the seams. We are caught, in Lukácsian phrase, between 'dead objectivity and vacuous subjectivity'.[10] The solidity of the realist character dissolves into a set of fragmentary mental states. Individuals are mutually isolated and stripped of their social relations, while history becomes either static, cyclical or directionless. With the loss of a genuinely historical sense, narrative buckles or simply collapses. Most of the finest literary artists of the twentieth century can thus be sent packing for failing to achieve a form of realism they never aimed for in the first place. In this sense, Lukács the political revolutionary comes up with a curiously traditionalist version of art. Treating the artwork as a seamless whole has a venerable history from Aristotle to the American New Critics.

A number of Marxist theorists, among them Theodor Adorno, have argued that abstraction is inherent to capitalism, given the sovereignty of the commodity form. The commodity is abstract in the sense that its material content is irrelevant to its value, which is determined simply by the act of exchange. So if reality itself is shot through with abstraction, why is an art which reflects this condition not to be judged realist? And if solitude and futility are the fate of the modern subject, why should an art which exemplifies this condition not be judged as truer than one which does not? The answer for Lukács is that art must do more than reflect its surroundings. It must bring to light their underlying historical significance; and it is this, he insists, that modernism is incapable of accomplishing. Far from resolving the conflict between the social and individual, modernist art simply reproduces it. At the same time, fragmentation begins to invade literary form itself, as it does in Eliot's *The Waste Land* and Pound's *The Cantos*. The work no longer presents us with a complex, well-integrated totality. Instead, it mirrors the way in which under capitalism, different features of the social whole are split off from each other and become reified as things in themselves.[11] One of Lukács's objections to modernist art is that it leaves conflicts unreconciled, which some might see as a more realist move than the method he advocates himself. The Hungarian Marxist critic József Révai rebukes his compatriot for this urge to unify, remarking that 'a writer does not become great by trying to "dissolve" and synthesise the opposites at any price. On the contrary, a writer often becomes great by revealing these opposites, or at least pointing out their irreconcilable character.'[12]

Realism for Lukács includes more than the novel from Scott to Tolstoy. It is a heritage of high art which stretches back to Aeschylus and Shakespeare. Its three major phases are ancient Greece, the Renaissance and early nineteenth-century France. So it is a universal category – indeed, the essence of all authentic art – but also a historically specific one. It is not clear that these two claims are compatible. If Lukács maintains as a Marxist that art springs from concrete historical conditions, how come realism persists across so many different periods? It is a curiously unhistorical standpoint for a historical materialist. Can Euripides's *Medea* and Walter Scott's *Waverley* really be squeezed into the same category? Marxist theory, to be sure, recognises a whole host of phenomena (labour, the state, ideology, exploitation) which are common to different historical periods; but these things take very different forms across the centuries, whereas Lukács's notion of realism remains remarkably constant from Sophocles to Stendhal.

On this theory, the content of realist fiction is historical, while its form is utopian. There is struggle, discord and upheaval, but they are contained by the formal unity of the work. It is as though literary form allows us a foretaste of a harmonious future. If this strikes a note of hope, however, it is a distinctly muted one. What, then, if realism represents one of the few forms of authentic humanity still to be found in the Stalinist wilderness? What if writing realist novels, of all minority pursuits, stands in for a genuine socialism which seems to have vanished from the historical agenda? Socialism aims to build a just and equal society, but to do so in a way that allows individual freedom and fulfilment to thrive. In a similar way, the realist novel constitutes a totality, but one which is achieved in and through its individual components. Stalinism, by contrast, achieves totality only by riding roughshod over the uniquely specific. In this sense, literary realism can act as a tacit critique of it. To praise Stendhal and Tolstoy becomes code for condemning the Soviet regime. It is also a smack at socialist realism, which was to become the official artistic line of the Soviet Union. Lukács was as hostile to this art form as he was to a supposedly decadent modernism, though for reasons of political prudence he refrained from calling it by its name during Stalin's reign. He also attacks it under cover of criticising bourgeois naturalism, which we shall be looking at later.

In *The Meaning of Contemporary Realism*, Lukács tips his hat to socialist realism but is sharply critical of much that passes for it. It is a form of art that has been much ridiculed, not least for its portraits of brawny workers straddling tractors while raising their careworn faces to a rose-coloured dawn. Yet it actually represented a less hard-line approach to art in the Soviet Union than had been the case with the previous cultural orthodoxy.

The custodian of this orthodoxy was the Russian Association of Proletarian Writers, whose Russian acronym, appropriately enough, was RAPP. Sectarian, dogmatic, militantly class-conscious and dismissive of well-meaning fellow travellers, RAPP and its supporters championed such projects as collective novel-writing on construction sites and factory floors, a prospect unlikely to gladden the heart of Salman Rushdie or Ian McEwan.

At the Soviet Writers' Congress of 1934, the new policy of socialist realism was officially unveiled. The anonymous introduction to a selection of the conference speeches proclaims with a straight face that while the Congress was in session, 'it is not too much to say that the whole Soviet Union, with all its millions of workers, concentrated its attention upon questions of literature'.[13] One can picture farm labourers resting on their spades for a couple of hours to debate the relative merits of Pushkin and Gogol. Despite declaring that bourgeois writing is finished and that Soviet literature is the finest in the world, most of the participants are prepared to be cautiously critical of the status quo. Proletarian writers must learn from the masters of language of critical realism, not least in matters of form and style. (The author Nikolai Tolstoy is rather more relaxed in this respect, claiming that 'we need not be afraid of clumsy and lengthy descriptions, or tedious characterisations: we need monumental realism!')[14]

A diversity of literary forms should be fostered, as long as writers remain loyal to the proletarian world-view. A purely photographic naturalism is to be rejected. Socialist realism is not a passive reflection of reality, but should look instead to a transformation of social consciousness. (It is worth noting that if the Soviet fiction of the time really had reflected the dire condition of the nation, it would not have secured the rubber stamp of the state.) In pursuing this task, socialist authors must draw on the cultural resources of all previous epochs, even if in Maxim Gorky's view the role of the middle classes in cultural creation has been greatly exaggerated. (Bourgeois literature, he bafflingly declares, began in ancient Egypt, Greece and Rome, and emerges again in feudal society.) Proletarian writing may foreshadow the future, but so far it has been woefully sparse and insufficient. Still, the bourgeoisie, given that it is in its death throes, is no longer capable of producing major art, unless its more dissident writers desert this camp for the cause of the working class.

In this respect, Karl Radek points proudly to a group of writers 'in the heart of bourgeois England, at Oxford', who realise 'that the only salvation lies in alliance with the proletariat'.[15] W.H. Auden and his poetic colleagues are held up as role models of the enlightened class traitor, in contrast to the 'fascist' T.S. Eliot. Without such shifts of political allegiance, the destiny of middle-class literature is 'to rot in the fascist dungeons, to putrefy in the cess pit of pornography, to wander in the shadows of mysticism'.[16] Proletarian literature may also serve to convince sceptical citizens of the need for severe measures in constructing socialism. Those who failed to grasp the need to liquidate the kulak (rich peasant) class, Radek enthuses, had been heard to declare after reading the novels of Mikhail Sholokhov: 'He has convinced me that it had to be that way.'[17]

All the same, the masters of critical realism still tower embarrassingly above the meagre offerings of proletarian art. In order to make progress, such art should renounce a narrow focus on class struggle and be open to the whole social process. It should attend to sentiment and psychology as well as to history and society. According to Nikolai Bukharin, 'the whole multiplicity of life' must find itself portrayed, not simply 'an elementary portrait, a beam to which a red flag is nailed'.[18] Abstract ideas must be clothed in tangible images. History must be portrayed in its dynamic development, not in some more static mode. Despite being visionary and heroic in its outlook, the brand of writing championed by the Congress is also sober, decent and primly moralistic. Its sensibility, in other words, is petty-bourgeois as well as proletarian. There will be no more degenerate novels in which the hero is a lascivious two-legged goat in trousers, promises Gorky. Neither will we see any more works like Joyce's *Ulysses* – 'a heap of dung, crawling with worms, photographed by a cinema apparatus through a microscope', as Karl Radek (who mistakes the year in which the work is set) thunders from the podium.[19]

Realism and naturalism

Despite Lukács's aversion to socialist realism, his own literary views are in some ways curiously close to it. Both he and the socialist realists denounce a narrowly class-based fiction; both are hostile to 'photographic' naturalism; both praise the masterpieces of bourgeois realism; both reject a purely diagrammatic art for a more inward, psychologised portrayal of character. Such, at least, was the socialist realist theory. When it came to the practice, however, Lukács, as we have seen, found this form of writing thoroughly objectionable, accusing it of some of the errors which he also found in literary naturalism. Both the socialist realist and naturalist novel were to be denounced as deviations from critical realism.

Broadly speaking, the naturalism of the late nineteenth century rests on the conviction that all phenomena are explicable in natural or scientific terms, without need to resort to spiritual, supernatural or (in the case of especially hard-nosed naturalists) psychological explanations. It is, in short, a form of materialism. In fact, in modern European history the two terms have sometimes been synonymous. Unlike realism, which refers to an artistic style, naturalism is more of a self-conscious movement. Among the writers associated with it are Flaubert, Zola, Maupassant, the Goncourt brothers, Ibsen, Shaw, Gissing, Strindberg, Theodore Dreiser, Jack London, Upton Sinclair, Arnold Bennett, John Galsworthy and H.G. Wells. The reader may note that this pantheon betrays a certain gender bias. The writer is a quasi-scientific observer of his surroundings, examining characters and events in dispassionate, severely objectivist style. What fascinates him is less human beings than the material, psychological and physiological laws which determine their behaviour. Realist writers may be emotionally engaged with the characters they create, and some, one suspects, may even be covertly in love with their heroes or heroines, but naturalism would dismiss this as a form of Romantic self-indulgence. An austere impersonality is the keynote. If art is unable to beat science, it can at least try to join it. The scientific spirit will now colonise the terrain which has traditionally proved most resistant to it: imaginative literature. The influence of photography is also apparent – though the word 'photographic', when applied to naturalistic fiction, usually means something like a neutral record of reality, which is hardly how most theorists of photography would regard the art.

'I am simply an observer who sets down facts', announces Emile Zola.[20] This, one might note, is not exactly the procedure of the scientist, who deals with facts, indeed establishes what counts as a fact, only within the context of a hypothesis. All the same, the writer in Zola's view is no mere passive spectator of the world. Instead, he is an experimenter who places his characters in a series of situations in order to record how they behave under the joint influences of heredity and environment. There is a curious echo here of Wordsworth and Coleridge's Preface to *Lyrical Ballads*, which speaks in proto-naturalistic spirit of the poet observing how men and women combine ideas in states of emotional excitement. It is as though the Lake District is converted into a laboratory. When Ralph Waldo Emerson exhorts his compatriots to 'replace sentimentalism by realism, and dare to uncover those simple and terrible laws which, be they seen or unseen, pervade and govern', he speaks like a naturalist.[21]

In Zola's view, naturalism is a continuation and completion of physiology. Like much of science, it contributes indirectly to the conquest of Nature and the exercise of human sovereignty over it. The point of dissecting the laws which govern the world is to make us masters of them. Women and men are products of their environment, but they are also capable of refashioning it. In promoting their power over Nature, the naturalistic novel is a functional rather than artistic affair. Indeed, it might well be described as anti-artistic. It is wary of the creative imagination and intent on purging all traces of Romantic idealism from its pages. 'The imagination no longer has a function', Zola declares triumphantly.[22] 'Capitalist prose,' laments Lukács, 'triumphed over the poetry of life.'[23] Flights of fancy give way to the patient collection of facts and the painstaking documentation of evidence. Case histories take over from moral situations, and temperament usurps character. The aim of the naturalists is not artistry but truth.[24] It is a time-honoured purpose of art, except for the fact that the truth at stake is now of a scientific kind.

In writing of this kind, so Lukács protests, human beings are reduced to biological organisms.[25] The individual gives way not to the type but to the specimen. At the same time, social reality is reified, treated as an unchangeable second nature. The dynamic relations between subjects and objects, which reach their highpoint in critical realism, are severed, leaving hollowed-out human beings confronting a lifeless world. Naturalist art regards individuals simply as the product of social, genetic, racial and temperamental factors. The idea of free human agency is accordingly rejected. Social existence is as strictly governed by laws as the physical world. 'One and the same determinism,' writes Zola, 'must govern the stone in the road and the brain of man.'[26] This is not the case with critical realism, which respects the distinction between culture and Nature, or psychology and physiology.

Naturalism is hardly notable for its rose-tinted vision of humanity. Beneath the brittle veneer of civilisation lurk certain bestial instincts and passions, which it is the task of the artist to record in scrupulously neutral style. Judgements such as good and bad, or beautiful and ugly, are purely subjective prejudices foisted upon a Nature which is blankly indifferent to them. Values are accordingly cut adrift from facts, or repudiated altogether. Art has no more truck with morality than does astrophysics. As Erich Auerbach complains,

> Objective seriousness which seeks to penetrate to the depths of the passions and entanglements of a human life, but without itself becoming moved, or at least without betraying that it is moved – this is an attitude which one expects from a priest, a teacher, or a psychologist rather than from an artist.[27]

The naturalistic artist no more passes moral judgement on his characters than a chemist does on a piece of manganese. His task is to portray the world around him without distorting or idealising it, rather than to approach his materials in critical or partisan spirit.

In any case, evolution has cut the ground from beneath conventional rankings. Who can tell what lowly organism might evolve in the fullness of time into some superb flourish of life? It is also true that the most trivial of actions can breed tragedies of Sophoclean proportions, as Thomas Hardy was aware. An egalitarianism of subject matter is thus established: rather as all citizens have a right to be politically represented, so whatever exists in the world, however foul or trite, is entitled to end up between the covers of a novel. Its moral or aesthetic ugliness is beside the point. In this respect, naturalism represents an extreme reaction to Romanticism. As the Goncourt brothers comment, 'Living in the nineteenth century, in a time of universal suffrage and democracy, of liberalism, we have asked ourselves whether those we have called "the lower classes" have not their right to the novel.'[28] One critic remarks of Gustave Flaubert that in democratic spirit he 'made all words equal just as he suppressed any hierarchy between worthy and unworthy subjects, between narration and description, foreground and background, and, ultimately, between men and things', a comment that could be applied to naturalism in general.[29] The American author William Dean Howells argues that fiction of this kind refuses to establish hierarchies, finding nothing insignificant but rather 'feel[ing] in every nerve the equality of things and the unity of men'.[30] It is a form of literary democracy as well as a species of pseudoscience. Rather as the right to vote is extended to the common people at the end of the nineteenth century, so, too, is middle-class realism. In its support of the humble and inconspicuous, naturalist artists could strike up close alliances with socialists and feminists.

Whereas critical realism tends to centre on exceptional figures, naturalist art is doggedly anti-heroic, preoccupied with the everyday rather than the remarkable. In Lukács's view, it is condemned to a purely external or mechanical approach to social reality. Unlike critical realism, it is unable to delve beneath the specious surfaces of social life in order to reveal its hidden truth. In Hegelian terms, it represents a 'bad immediacy'. Theodor Adorno, using the term 'realism' for what Lukács would call naturalism, declares that

The reactionary nature of any realist aesthetic today is inseparable from its commodity character. Tending to reinforce, affirmatively, the phenomenal surface of society, realism dismissed any attempt to penetrate that surface as a romantic endeavour.[31]

The politics of naturalism are ambiguous. Even if it abandons the critical thrust of the great realists, it is by no means congenial to the clean-living middle classes. An English newspaper of 1881 speaks of 'that unnecessary portrayal of offensive incidents for which M. Zola has found the new name of "Naturalism"'.[32] Flaubert's *Madame Bovary*, a work which anticipates naturalism proper, was widely condemned as immoral and the author himself was prosecuted. At the time, the offending literary label was not naturalism but realism. The French painter Gustave Courbet came under fire from the art establishment for his portrayal of peasants and labourers, and issued manifestoes on realism as a form of counter-attack. When the Paris Exposition of 1855 refused to hang his pictures, he set up his own pavilion of realism in retaliation. Denounced as a socialist and anti-clericalist, he took part in the Paris Commune of 1871 and was packed off into exile.

Since naturalism regards the whole of experience as grist to its artistic mill, it is at home in an urban underworld of lust, violence and destitution, one discreetly suppressed by polite society. Henrik Ibsen's play *Ghosts*, which deals with hereditary syphilis, was banned throughout most of Europe, and one critic records that when it was staged in London, 'the outpouring of critical venom it aroused has scarcely been equalled in theatre history'.[33] The play survived in the English capital for only one performance. Naturalism in general provoked howls of moral horror from the guardians of middle-class morality, who viewed it as gross, nauseating and morally repugnant. The fastidious Henry James, who rightly notes the relative lack of sprightliness, wit and humour in naturalistic fiction, finds Zola's novel *L'Assommoir* pervaded by a ferociously bad smell like an emanation from an open drain.[34] The so-called kitchen sink dramatists of the 1950s and 1960s were to elicit much the same disgust.

Such outrage, to adopt an epigram of Oscar Wilde, represents the rage of the philistine bourgeois at seeing his own face in the glass.[35] Even so, the characters we encounter in the works of Zola and his colleagues are not for the most part Dickensian clerks or Jamesian heiresses but miners, sex workers, alcoholics, petty thugs, impoverished shop assistants and tight-fisted peasants. The whole class basis of the novel begins to shift, as the urban proletariat and poor peasantry move centre stage. Yet they are presented more as objects of study than as social agents. Some naturalists, influenced by Social Darwinism and theories of heredity, regarded the poor as closer to the animal kingdom than their more civilised superiors. If the grossness of naturalism is abhorrent to middle-class readers, its demeaning attitude to the common people could prove rather more acceptable.

In its blending of the clinical and the sensational, this brand of fiction can border on the pornographic. It is an art which is at once sober and scandalous. One might see it as a kind of realism to the second power, more militant and programmatic than anything to be found in George Eliot or Leo Tolstoy. Fiction is no longer a mannered, morally edifying affair. The real is now what hurts – whatever is grotesque, repulsive, misshapen or pathological. Value lies not in the literary materials themselves, but in the scrupulous means by which the author represents them. And if this is so, then naturalism risks flipping over into formalism.

The school had its contemporary critics. Marcel Proust claims that a literature which does no more than list and describe, despite its pretensions to realism, lies at the furthest possible remove from reality.[36] Oscar Wilde regards both realism and naturalism as shameful betrayals of the artistic spirit. In his essay 'The Decay of Lying', he complains of those authors who 'fall into careless habits of accuracy', developing 'a morbid and unhealthy faculty of truth-telling'.[37] We must put an end to the monstrous worship of facts, which is usurping the realm of fancy and vulgarising humankind. Art does not hold up a mirror to life. On the contrary, it is art that is real and life that tries blunderingly to imitate it. 'Where, if not from the Impressionists,' Wilde asks, his tongue thrust deeply in his cheek, 'do we get those wonderful brown fogs that come creeping down our streets, blurring the gas-lamps and changing the houses into monstrous shadows?'[38] 'No great artist ever sees things as they are', he insists. 'If he did, he would cease to be an artist.'[39] 'All bad art,' he continues, 'comes from returning to Life and Nature, and elevating them into Ideals.'[40]

The account of naturalism I have just sketched is in some ways a purist version of the doctrine. There is a good deal more to Zola or Ibsen, as Lukács himself concedes, than the conversion of men and women into mere creatures of appetite, or the reduction of art to the purely mimetic. In fact, naturalistic art is often most effective when it breaks with its own beliefs, as the author momentarily forgets to pose as a surgeon or sociologist. All the same, Lukács is right to see it as deviating from the realism he prizes so highly. Its preoccupation with the diseased and degenerate represents a major shift of sensibility. It is as though the criterion of the real is now the ugly, while beauty and harmony are dim memories of a faded Romantic era.

Lukács regards naturalism as the flipside of modernism. He sees it as a falsely objectivist form of art, in contrast to such falsely subjectivist ones as Expressionism and Surrealism. Neither can penetrate the surface of social life to reveal the historical forces at work beneath it. 'The realist,' Lukács insists in grimly prescriptive mood, 'must seek out the lasting features in people, in their relations with each other and in the situations in which they have to act; he must focus on those elements which endure over long periods and which constitute the objective human tendencies of society and indeed of mankind as a whole.'[41] Given a change of style, this statement could have been made by Samuel Johnson. There is an embarrassing accord between the twentieth-century Marxist and the eighteenth-century neo-classicist.

Lukács's chief antagonist in this respect is the poet and playwright Bertolt Brecht, who points to the irony of a Marxist critic nostalgic for the art of the nineteenth century. 'Be like Balzac – only up to date!' is Brecht's sardonic summary of

Lukács's case.[42] Lukács may accuse the modernists of a sterile formalism; but it is his own brand of realism, Brecht insists, which is truly formalistic. It seeks to preserve outmoded literary forms in lofty indifference to historical change. 'Literary works cannot be taken over like factories', he argues. 'Literary forms of expression cannot be taken over like patents.'[43] To copy the great critical realists in very different historical conditions means ceasing to be realist. If reality itself changes, then so must one's means of representing it. 'We must not conjure up a kind of Valhalla of the enduring figures of literature,' Brecht warns, 'a kind of Madame Tussaud's panopticon, filled with nothing but durable characters from Antigone to Nana and from Aeneas to Nekhlyudov (who is he, by the way?)'.[44] The traditional conception of character will alter as socialism itself evolves.

Realism for Lukács is a question of technique; but it is the only technique which will give you access to the truth. Brecht agrees that the task of realism is to reveal how things stand with the world, but he does not believe that there is only one method by which to achieve this goal. On the contrary, realist art can use whatever procedures it finds most fruitful: shock, montage, song, film, documentation, fragmentation, discontinuity, interior monologue, the use of technology, popular cultural forms and the like. Realist representation is not always a radical move. Putting a factory on stage, Brecht comments, will tell you nothing about capitalism. There is no reason why socialist art should be realist art, as the Soviet ideologues assume. Many an experimental artist of the early twentieth century, from the Dadaists and Futurists to the Constructivists and Surrealists, were either Communist party members or loyal fellow travellers, but they had little time for straightforward representation. What was the point of reflecting a social reality which was about to be overtaken by the future? And how would reproducing the way things are help to change them? Brecht reports that the working people who attend his theatre in Berlin welcome its non-realist approaches, and would no doubt be reluctant to plough their way through the work of realists like Scott or Pushkin. One must begin from the bad new days, not the good old ones. Perry Anderson points out that Brecht's theatre 'represents perhaps the only major body of art produced after the Russian revolution to be uncompromisingly advanced in form, yet intransigently popular in intention'.[45]

'With the people struggling and changing reality before our eyes,' Brecht writes with a cold eye on Lukács,

we must not cling to 'tried' rules of narrative, venerable literary models, eternal aesthetic laws. We must not derive realism as such from particular existing works, but we shall use every means, old and new, tried and untried, derived from art and derived from other sources, to render reality to men in a form they can master.[46]

Non-realist methods can be harnessed to realist ends. What matters is getting at the truth, not the means you use to do so.

There is, however, at least one respect in which Brecht comes off unfavourably in contrast with his Hungarian colleague. When the workers of East Germany rose up against their Stalinist rulers in 1953, Brecht's reaction was a truculent defence of the government, whereas Lukács, as we have seen already, bravely took part in a similar uprising in Hungary three years later and was driven into exile as a result.

One problem with the term 'realism' is that it can be both descriptive and evaluative. It can mean a specific mode of representation, without implying any particular judgement on it; or it can suggest that a work is true to life, and that this is a virtue in itself. In Lukács's eyes, the two senses of the word are inseparable. You can be true to life only through a specific way of representing it. 'Art always aims at the representation of Reality, i.e. of Truth,' proclaims the Victorian author G.H. Lewes, 'and no departure from truth is permissible, except such as inevitably lies in the nature of the medium itself.'[47] But Lewes does not say whether truth and reality can be revealed only by a particular artistic approach, which is what Lukács has in mind. For Brecht, a work is realist if its effect is to enlighten its audience about the nature of social reality. This implies that a play or poem might turn out to be realist in one context but not in another. Realism for Brecht is a relational term. It involves a dialogue between work and reader. An image may be realist in the sense of depicting the familiar world, but so feeble or hackneyed that it has no genuine impact on readers or audiences. In Brecht's homely phrase, an audience must be able to get something out of it. Works of art can be both lifelike and lifeless.

If realism is an evaluative term, meaning something like 'a convincing portrayal of reality', then art works which are formally non-realist may still lay claim to the title – *Waiting for Godot* or *Where the Wild Things Are*, for example. The trouble with this inclusive definition is that it threatens to stretch the term 'realism' beyond any useful meaning. Is any art that genuinely affects an audience to be called realist? The French critic Roger Garaudy expands the concept to include art works from 'the friezes of Phidias to the mosaics of Ravenna, from Poussin to Cézanne or Picasso'.[48] Harry Levin insists that 'all great writers, in so far as they are committed to a searching and scrupulous critique of life as they know it, may be reckoned among the realists'.[49] Would only bad art then count as non-realist? In the Soviet Union of the 1920s, almost every artistic movement, however audaciously experimental, laid claim to the title of realism. This was one reason why the Nazis refused to use the label for their own art even when it was plainly representational.[50] 'New realism', 'heroic realism', 'revolutionary realism' and (in 1920s Germany) the so-called New Objectivity, all drew on the concept to legitimate an art which was sometimes far from representational. Used in this elastic way, the word simply becomes a synonym for 'effective' or 'illuminating'. Like any term that can cover almost anything, it means almost nothing. Friedrich Nietzsche maintained that realism in art was an illusion because all artists are convinced that they exemplify it.

Perhaps, then, there is a distinction to be made between 'realist' and 'realistic' – the former meaning a true-to-life style of representation, and the latter describing a work of art's power to persuade. Charles Baudelaire dismisses realism as 'rustic, coarse, dishonest and even boorish' while declaring almost in the same breath that 'every good poet was always realistic'.[51] The claim need not be self-contradictory. Many avant-garde artists would accept that their work is formally speaking non-realist, while being rather less gratified to be told that it is unrealistic in the sense of being thin, vacuous and a grotesque travesty of human existence. If realism means the opposite of the latter, it is hard to think of an author who would not lay claim to the title. But this, as we have just seen, is part of the problem.

5

REALISM AND THE COMMON LIFE

The value of the commonplace

One difference between celebrities and the rest of humanity is that whereas celebrities lead humdrum lives in addition to the more glamorous aspects of their existence (they need to pull on their own socks, for example, unless they happen to be King Charles), the great majority lead nothing *but* everyday lives. Nobody in Patagonia will be aware of the names they give their children, their houses will not be overrun by hordes of inquisitive tourists and if they are mobbed in the street it is only because they are mistaken for shoplifters. It is these men and women, by and large, who are the stuff of realist fiction, along with the odd haughty aristocrat or swashbuckling hero. Among other things, the realist novel helps to establish everyday human experience, not least its domestic aspects, as a valid sphere of investigation, and a richly rewarding one at that. As Franco Moretti comments, the novel 'has produced a phenomenology that makes normality interesting and mean-ingful *as* normality'.[1] Its stomping ground, according to Mikhail Bakhtin, is 'the open public spaces of public squares, streets, cities and villages'.[2]

There is, then, a bond between realism and the common people, which is not true of the literary forms which flour-ished previously. 'Populace' here means not just the working class but extends to the lower and middling middle classes as well, from Gulliver and Robinson Crusoe to David Cop-perfield and Dorothea Brooke. In fact, one might claim that literary realism is born when middle-class society begins to find its own everyday experience a source of endless fascina-tion. It also begins to decline when the value and solidity of that experience is called into question. It is hard to overesti-mate the revolutionary nature of an art which takes socially inconspicuous women and men with complete seriousness, rather than simply allotting them walk-on parts as maidser-vants or innkeepers. It is one of the genuinely innovative features of literary realism, as we shall see in a moment in the work of Erich Auerbach.

Another such feature is the belief that commonplace things have value in themselves, not simply as aids to salvation or as allegories of a higher truth. The origin of this turn to the fa-miliar, it has been argued, is to be found in Christianity. The Acts of the Apostles describes St Peter and St John as ordinary, uneducated men. Jesus may be a tragic figure, but he is not a heroic one. He is presented as a vagrant from the rural backwater of Galilee, without home, money, property or profession. He has a family, but seems fairly indifferent to it. For the New Testament, it is the common life which is the locus of salvation, not some sacred cult or consecrated place. God is an animal, the Word made flesh, in whose person the humble and the sublime are conjoined. What the Father demands is not burnt offerings but mercy and justice. According to St Luke's Gospel, his presence is to be felt wherever the poor are filled with good things and the rich are sent empty away.

The philosopher Charles Taylor, who speaks of the Christian 'affirmation of ordinary life',[3] sketches a transition from a medieval age of military prowess and aristocratic honour to the middle-class Protestant or Puritan ethic of modern times. This Protestant ethic, Taylor argues, 'displaces the locus of the good life from some special range of higher activities and places it within "life" itself. The self-fulfilling human life is now defined in terms of labour and production, on the one hand, and marriage and family life, on the other.'[4] Notions of blood and nobility give way to the civic and vocational. What matters now are the spheres of work, domesticity and material acquisition. In a reversal of values, labour is granted a dignity previously denied it, while married love is exalted over erotic escapades and romantic imbroglios. It is from this historic shift that the modern realist novel arises. We are in the presence of what George Eliot in *Adam Bede* calls the faithful representing of common things. It is a type of art which would probably have been inconceivable to Sophocles and scandalous to Pope and Racine.

The Reformation sets about dismantling the distinction between the sacred and the secular, so that everyday society becomes the arena of salvation or damnation. One consequence of this blurring of borders is an intense concern with the details of daily existence, in the most trifling features of which one may detect the signs of God's wrath or favour. There is also a preoccupation with the individual, who now confronts his Maker in fearful solitude, without the mediation of a priestly caste. And since all men and women are equal in the eyes of their Creator, an aggressive individualism is laced with a measure of democracy and egalitarianism. All this is reflected in realist writing. If one adds a distaste for ritual, hierarchy and tradition, it is not too fanciful to describe realist fiction as a Protestant form. Plot, which will finally grant the characters their punishments or rewards, takes the place of divine Providence.

Auerbach's realist vision

The claim that literary realism has its roots in Judaeo-Christianity is a prominent feature of Erich Auerbach's magisterial study *Mimesis: The Representation of Reality in Western Literature* (1946), a work widely considered to be the finest ever published on the subject. Auerbach begins by contrasting Homeric epic with the Hebrew Scriptures, noting that there is an individual flavour about characters in the Bible which is lacking in Homer.

They can evolve in their inner lives, unlike the relatively static figures of ancient epic. It is the difference between history and legend, whatever the non-historical nature of much of the Jewish Scriptures. Legend tends to neglect precise details of time and place and presents the reader with largely unambiguous meanings. The narrative is stripped of all that is fraught, uncertain and unresolved. History, by contrast, is a question of conflicts and cross-currents – of multiple, ambiguous events which resist being neatly schematised. What we have, in effect, are two different linguistic registers – the 'high style' of myth, epic and romance, which belongs largely to a class of warriors and noblemen, and a more popular idiom.

The point, however, is not that Homeric epic is sublime while the Hebrew Scriptures are prosaic. We have noted already that the Judaeo-Christian tradition mingles high and low, with the result that for Auerbach 'the sublime, tragic and problematic take shape precisely in the domestic and commonplace'.[5] Few biblical passages are more striking in this respect (though Auerbach happens not to allude to it) than the twenty-fifth chapter of Matthew's Gospel, which presents Jesus as returning to earth on clouds of glory only for us to discover that entry to his kingdom depends on nothing more exalted than feeding the hungry and visiting the sick. It is an artfully contrived moment of bathos, rather like the Messiah riding into Jerusalem on a donkey. For Auerbach, the Christian era is marked by a clash of different styles, and so is the realist novel.

In antiquity, by contrast, these two kinds of language are kept sharply distinct. Auerbach observes in *Mimesis* (p. 31) of ancient literature:

> Everything commonly realistic, everything pertaining to everyday life, must not be treated on any level except the comic . . . we are forced to conclude that there could be no serious literary treatment of everyday occupations and social classes – merchants, artisans, peasants, slaves – home, shop, field, store – of everyday customs and institutions – marriage, children, work, earning a living – in short, of the people and its life.

Only with the advent of the modern age could a washed-up American salesman be treated as a tragic figure. There is a link in ancient works between this aloofness from the common life and a lack of historical consciousness, for

> It is precisely in the intellectual and economic conditions of everyday life that those forces are revealed which underlie historical movements; these, whether military, diplomatic, or related to the inner constitution of the state, are only the product, the final result, of variants in the depths of everyday life.   (p. 33)

This is not far from Lukács, though there are also key differences. Whereas Lukács is a Marxist, Auerbach is a populist for whom it is the multitude, in all its verve and diversity, which lies at the heart of historical development. In his judgement, Christianity is exemplary of this 'birth of a spiritual movement in the depths of the common people' (p. 43). He notes with relish the outraged response of some 'highly educated pagans' of classical antiquity to the scandal that 'the highest truths were contained in writings composed in a language to their mind impossibly uncivilised and in total ignorance of the stylistic categories' (p. 154). The laconic idiom of the Gospels, addressed to illiterate peasants, fishermen and the like, is indeed remote from the realm of fine writing.

Mimesis records the history of Western representations of reality, but it is a more partisan survey than one might expect. There is a clear distaste for the kind of literary art (epic, heroic or neo-classical) which invites its readers to admire 'a distant world, whose instincts and ideals . . . evolve in uncompromising purity and freedom, in comparison with the friction and resistance of real life' (p. 121). Literary works which are schematic, idealising, rigid in structure and socially restricted are awarded a low rating. Courtly and chivalric art, for example, is a hindrance to the full apprehension of reality. There is a preference for less stylised, more earth-bound forms of writing. It is no wonder that Auerbach is an admirer of Montaigne, 'the dignity of (whose) subject matter never makes him renounce an earthy popular turn of expression or an image taken from everyday life' (p. 309). Intellectual seriousness and an unbuttoned conversational ease sit comfortably together.

By contrast with a stiffly formalist art, Dante looms up as a magnificent realist, with a style

> so immeasurably richer in directness, vigour, and subtlety [than his predecessor poets] . . . he knows and uses such an immeasurably greater stock of forms, he expresses the most varied phenomena and subjects with such immeasurably superior firmness and assurance, that we come to the conclusion that this man used his language to discover the world anew.   (pp. 182–3)

'Nowhere does the mingling of styles', Auerbach comments, 'come so close to the violation of all style' (p. 185), as the unremarkable and monstrously disfigured are to be found cheek-by-jowl with the loftiest truths. Realist prose is both vulgar and sublime. Rabelais is another author who foreshadows modern realism, breaking with the unified form of some late medieval works for what amounts to artistic anarchy. 'In Rabelais,' Auerbach enthuses, 'there is no aesthetic standard; everything goes with everything' (p. 278).

For all his prefiguring of realism, however, Dante remains traditional enough to treat earthly things as figures of eternity. Divine truth in his poetry is both eternal and time-bound. His poetry may be vulgar or grotesque in places, but even his grotesquerie can be couched in an elevated style. The literary realism of the modern period will shed this rhetoric while retaining its commonplace content. In the meanwhile, however, there is the towering figure of Shakespeare, who even in the 'high' mode of tragedy is not averse to 'mentioning everyday utensils' or 'the everyday processes of life' (p. 313). The tragic and comic, majestic and mundane, rub shoulders in his work, while characters are more richly depicted than in the drama of the ancients. His expansive social range is also favourably contrasted with the less varied scope of most of his predecessors. Even so, there are limits to Shakespearian realism – traces of the supernatural, for example, or the fact that his tragic protagonists are invariably of noble birth.

Stendhal, Balzac and Flaubert all display what Auerbach takes to be the two primary features of literary realism: a serious treatment of everyday life, not least of characters drawn from the lower social strata, and a keen sense of social and historical circumstance. The final chapter of his book is devoted to Virginia Woolf, on whom it passes a resoundingly negative judgement. Indeed, Auerbach finds little in modernist writing to applaud. Joyce, he is candid enough to confess, has him completely beaten. He dislikes non-realist experiment, which he condemns as formless, unhistorical and excessively gloomy. The judgement is as doctrinaire as anything in Lukács. Auerbach, the champion of the fluid, humble and hybrid, turns out to be surprisingly rigid in his literary tastes.

For all its flexibility, Auerbach's use of the term 'realism' is not pointlessly open-ended. It does not mean any art which has a genuine impact, but neither does it capitulate to Lukács's straitlaced orthodoxy. Realism in Auerbach's view is a specific literary mode: concrete, fluid, precisely specified, diverse, open-ended, socially inclusive, historically minded, populist in spirit, respectful of the individual and distrustful of abstract ideas and rigid programmes. Yet rather than being confined to a particular period or genre, it crops up all the way from the Book of Genesis to Emile Zola. Apart from the occasional lapse into Romantic, mythical and classical modes (Goethe comes in for some particularly rough treatment in this respect), Western literature is by and large the story of an ever richer, more intricate realism, at least until the arrival of modernism. It is a tale of historical progress or Whig theory of fiction. 'The spine of *Mimesis*,' writes that most ardent of Auerbachians, Edward Said, 'is the passage from the separation of styles in classical antiquity, to their mingling in the New Testament, their first great climax in Dante's *Divine Comedy*, and their ultimate apotheosis in the French realistic authors of the nineteenth century.'[6]

That this is also a political allegory is plain enough. Realism develops hand-in-glove with the growing power of the common people. When Auerbach wrote his book, the dismantling of popular democracy was a prominent feature of the Nazi regime from which, as a German Jew, he took refuge in Turkey. The heroic, hierarchical, mythological literature he finds unsettling is echoed in the art and ideology of Nazism. Realism, by contrast, would seem an inherently anti-fascist form. Written in exile in Istanbul between 1942 and 1945, *Mimesis* is as much a coded response to fascism as Lukács's praise of critical realism is a covert critique of Stalinism. In fact, Auerbach's work ends on a quasi-utopian note, all the more remarkable in light of the conditions in which it was produced. 'It is still a long way to a common life of mankind on earth,' Auerbach concedes, 'but the goal begins to be visible. And it is most concretely visible now in the unprejudiced, precise, interior and exterior representation of the random moment in the lives of different people' (p. 552). This declaration of faith is as poignant as it is impressive. If genuine community is to be found chiefly in realist art, then the political implications are cheerless indeed. Like Lukács, Auerbach hopes to keep the revolution warm by cherishing a certain strain of literary art. It is an alarmingly fragile foundation on which to build a future.

For post-Romantics like Auerbach, the concrete and changeable are inherently superior to the abstract and static. Nothing could be more alien to the modern sensibility than a refusal of this priority. Yet mutability, as we have seen already, is not always to be affirmed. One hopes that the public will continue to take the view that academics of advanced years should not be taken out and shot. Nor should the specific always be preferred to the general, even though this prejudice was one reason why Plato expelled poets from his ideal republic. Would *Waiting for Godot* have profited from providing Vladimir and Estragon with surnames, careers, hobbies, home towns and views on the rate of inflation? General ideas such as justice, gender, equality and patriarchy may prove essential for political change, while too myopic an outlook may obstruct it.

One might question, then, Auerbach's impatience with what he calls 'abstract and general forms of cognition' (p. 444). Piet Mondrian produced abstract paintings, but one would not protest too loudly at being given a couple to hang on one's wall. Mathematics is a highly abstract form of knowledge, but without it civilisation would be sunk. The most inimitable of individuals must be described in language which is common to us all. The utterly unique would lie beyond the frontiers of speech, a fact which has depressed a number of Romantic poets. The ability to generalise is part of the edge we have over most of our fellow animals, even if it can breed catastrophic effects as well as constructive ones. Auerbach also seems to regard the common people as somehow more substantial than the upper classes; but there are more compelling reasons for objecting to princes than the suspicion that they are less real than butchers. One might also wonder whether appealing to the populace as a counter to Romanticism and idealism is a piece of Romantic idealism.

Readers of the Russian theorist Mikhail Bakhtin will no doubt be struck by the parallels between his and Auerbach's arguments. For both critics, realism is an essentially bathetic form, puncturing the inflated oratory of a genteel class with the workaday wisdom of its underlings. For Auerbach, a populist art is preferable to a highly stylised one; for Bakhtin, the novel turns from official forms of discourse to the vibrant language of the marketplace. In his case, too, there are political issues at stake. His celebration of the novel is a covert polemic against Stalinism – a despotism to which he was eventually to fall victim himself.

Realism and postmodernism

We have seen that realism first sees the light of day in medieval Europe as a belief in the existence of universals. Paradoxically, however, it ends up in the modern period meaning just the opposite. While the European middle class is still in the ascendant, it regards itself as in principle a universal formation, intent on establishing its sovereignty over the planet as a whole. It is a dream which is finally realised in our own time. Yet the more capitalism extends its global sway, the more opaque, disjointed and unfathomable it becomes, which means the less it can be represented as a whole. As a result, the focus for many writers shifts from the overall vision to the sensuously specific. What is real is what one can taste, touch and smell. One of the keynotes of modern fiction can be found in Henry James's remark that 'the air of reality (solidity of specification) seems to me to be the supreme virtue of a novel'.[7]

At the same time, the scholastic doctrines of the medieval era give way to the empiricism of the modern age. Disdainful of abstractions, the practically-minded middle classes believe primarily in what they can buy and sell. Realism comes to mean the concrete and individual, rather than the notion of universal natures. The word has revolved on its axis, as realism in the scholastic sense is eclipsed by realism in its everyday meaning. 'Everything that exists is particular',[8] declares the philosopher George Berkeley's Philonus – to which Hegel and Marx might riposte that whether this is true or not, the particular is constituted by its relations to other particulars.

What is the fate of realism in a postmodern age? If critical realism can place too gullible a faith in order and stability, postmodernism overreacts to this conviction by viewing the world as infinitely malleable. Whereas realism finds normality interesting *as* normality, postmodern culture tends to look upon norms as restrictive and oppressive. What excites the postmodern mind is what deviates from the orthodox and consensual. This overlooks the fact that it is orthodox in modern societies to nurse the sick rather than to leave them to rot on rubbish dumps. Transgressing conventions includes rape and genocide as well as shocking suburbanites. There is also a consensus that people should not be denied civil rights because of their ethnicity. Postmodern thought is too captivated by the marginal and off-beat to find the life of the majority anything but uncool. In this context, the realist novel, as an incomparable phenomenology of the everyday, may serve to remind us of just how precious the commonplace can be.[9]

There are other reasons for postmodernism's wariness of realism. Since contemporary civilisation is permeated by signs and icons, why represent what is an image in any case? Besides, realism depends on a distinction between truth and fiction, which in some circles is now as quaintly outdated as circulating the snuff box. And don't things change so rapidly in this fluid form of life that they defeat representation altogether? Classical realism thrives on a degree of stability and continuity, neither of which are conspicuous features of the advanced capitalist world. Its characters have a consistency of identity which is foreign to the shopping mall or public relations industry. We are speaking of a transition in Western capitalism, as the system moves from production to consumption, the industrial to the post-industrial, coal mines to call centres, the sturdily unified self to the diffuse, desiring one.

Realism tends to trade on a distinction between surface appearance and hidden depth, a model which postmodernism rejects. Depth in its view is the place where fraudulent metaphysical ideas can germinate. Realist narratives are also too linear for the postmodern sensibility, which delights in space rather than time and has profound misgivings about the idea of progress. The past is converted into a repertoire of styles and modes to be plundered by the present, while the hope for a transformed future becomes an idle vision. The future will be much like the present, only with a more enticing array of options.

All the same, literary realism lives on, as though unaware of these adverse conditions. In fact, it remains the staple literary diet of millions of people who have little patience with images which they regard as untrue to life. In this sense, postmodern culture is by no means a wall-to-wall affair. Given our unflagging curiosity about ourselves, realism is perhaps the most tenacious art form that history has ever witnessed. It is true, as the avant-gardists never cease to admonish, that such unseemly eagerness to view our own face in the mirror can easily lapse into the pathology of narcissism. Yet it is not only our own visage which is in question. In an unfathomably complex world beset by terrorism and genocide, war, disease, poverty, mass migration and the gradual death of Nature, one of our most pressing needs is to grasp the overall shape of what is afoot. One of the tasks of realism, whether as fiction, documentary or reportage, is to provide us with this cognitive mapping, and to do so more enjoyably than most other forms of global knowledge.

ENDNOTES

1 GETTING REAL

1. Aristotle, *Rhetoric* (New York, 2010), p. 50.
2. See Benoit Peeters, *Derrida: A Biography* (Cambridge, 2012), p. 197.
3. Quoted by Harry Levin, *The Gates of Horn* (New York, 1966), p. 40.
4. See Gianni Vattimo, *Beyond Interpretation* (Cambridge, 1997) and *Nihilism and Emancipation* (New York, 2004).
5. Sabina Lovibond, *Reason and Imagination in Ethics* (Oxford, 1983), p. 9.
6. Charles Taylor, *The Ethics of Authenticity* (Cambridge, MA, 2018), p. 37.
7. Justus Buchler (ed.), *Philosophical Writings of Peirce* (New York, 1955), p. 79.
8. Richard Rorty, *Consequences of Pragmatism* (Minneapolis, MN, 1982), p. 166.
9. Hilary Putnam, *Reason, Truth and History* (Cambridge, 1981), p. 119.
10. Simon Blackburn, *Truth: A Guide for the Perplexed* (London, 2005), p. xviii.
11. Kwame Anthony Appiah, *The Ethics of Identity* (Princeton, NJ, 2005), p. 248.
12. Malcolm Bull, *Things Hidden* (London, 1999), pp. 49–50.
13. See Donald Davidson, 'On the Very Idea of a Conceptual Scheme', in *Inquiries into Truth and Interpretation* (Oxford, 1984).
14. The case is argued (with a few concessions here and there to relativism) by Paul O'Grady in his outstandingly lucid, compact study *Relativism* (Chesham, 2002).

15. See Thomas Nagel, *The View from Nowhere* (New York, 1986), p. 144.
16. Christopher Norris, 'Realism and Anti-Realism in Contemporary Philosophy', in Matthew Beaumont (ed.), *Adventures in Realism* (Oxford, 2007), p. 242. See also Roy Bhaskar, *Scientific Realism and Human Emancipation* (London, 1986). For a particularly fine discussion of realism, see Cora Diamond, *The Realistic Spirit* (Cambridge, MA, 1991), Ch. 1.
17. O'Grady, *Relativism*, p. 57.
18. See Blackburn, *Truth*, p. 176.
19. For an anti-realist case, see Richard Rorty, *Philosophy and the Mirror of Nature* (Oxford, 1980), *Objectivity, Relativism and Truth* (Cambridge, 1991) and *Contingency, Irony and Solidarity* (Cambridge, 1992). If I devote more space here to the realist rather than anti-realist case, it is partly because some rough-and-ready version of the latter is common in cultural circles today, whereas the former has had rather less of an airing.
20. Classic accounts of prescriptivism can be found in R.M. Hare, *The Language of Morals* (Oxford, 1952) and *Moral Thinking* (Oxford, 1981), especially Ch. 4.
21. Roger Scruton, *Modern Philosophy: A Survey* (London, 1994), pp. 279–80.
22. Stephen Mulhall, *Stanley Cavell: Philosophy's Recounting of the Ordinary* (Oxford, 2006), p. 80.
23. Lovibond, *Reason and Imagination in Ethics*, p. 1.
24. Alasdair MacIntyre, *After Virtue* (London, 1982), p. 57.
25. See Friedrich Engels, 'On Socialist Realism', in George J. Becker (ed.), *Documents of Modern Literary Realism* (Princeton, NJ, 1963) p. 485.
26. Iris Murdoch, *The Sovereignty of Good* (London and New York, 2006), p. 37.
27. Ibid., p. 39.
28. Ibid., p. 85.
29. Ibid.
30. Rodney Livingstone, 'Introduction', in György Lukács, *Essays on Realism* (London, 1980), p. 21.

2 WHAT IS REALISM? (1)

1. M.A.R. Habib, *A History of Literary Criticism* (Oxford, 2005), p. 471.
2. George Eliot, review of John Ruskin's *Modern Painters*, in *Westminster Review* no. lxv (April, 1856), p. 626.

3. Ian Watt, *The Rise of the Novel* (Harmondsworth, 1972). For another classic commentary on literary realism, see René Wellek, 'The Concept of Realism in Literary Scholarship', in Stephen J. Nichols Jr (ed.), *Concepts of Criticism* (New Haven and London, 1963).

4. Watt, *The Rise of the Novel*, p. 11.

5. Ibid., p. 32.

6. W.J.B. Owen and Jane Worthington Smyser (eds), *The Prose Works of William Wordsworth* (Oxford, 1974), vol. 1, p. 123.

7. André Breton, 'The First Manifesto of Surrealism', in J.H. Matthews (ed.), *Surrealism and the Novel* (Ann Arbor, MI, 1966), p. 1.

8. T.S. Eliot, 'Four Elizabethan Dramatists', in *T.S. Eliot: Selected Essays* (London, 1963), p. 111.

9. Levin, *The Gates of Horn*, p. 38.

10. See Fredric Jameson, *Signatures of the Visible* (New York and London, 1992), p. 166.

11. Karl Marx, 'Manifesto of the Communist Party', in *Marx and Engels: Selected Works* (London, 1968), p. 38.

12. Ibid.

13. See Jameson, *Signatures of the Visible*, p. 158.

14. Horace, *The Art of Poetry* (New York, 1974), p. 318.

15. Roman Jakobson, 'On Realism in Art', in *Language in Literature* (Cambridge, MA, and London, 1987), p. 20. For a valuable, wide-ranging survey of realism in general, see Pam Morris, *Realism* (London, 2003).

16. The essay can be found in Rachel Bowlby (ed.), *The Crowded Dance of Modern Life* (Harmondsworth, 1993).

17. Freud discusses these matters in *Beyond the Pleasure Principle* (Standard Edition of the Works of Sigmund Freud, London, 1955, vol. 18) and *The Ego and the Id* (Standard Edition, London, 1961, vol. 19).

18. For perhaps the finest philosophical study of this subject, see Kendall L. Walton, *Mimesis as Make-Believe* (Cambridge, MA, 1990).

19. Jameson, *Signatures of the Visible*, p. 166.

20. 'Maupassant on Realism as "Illusionism"', in Lilian Furst (ed.), *Realism* (London and New York, 1992), p. 46.

21. Henry James, 'The Future of the Novel', in *Henry James: Selected Literary Fiction* (Harmondsworth, 1963), p. 227.

22. John Lyon (ed.), *Henry James: Selected Tales* (London, 2001).

23. Ibid., p. 209.

24. Ibid., p. 218.

25. Ibid., p. 215.

26. Ibid., p. 214.

27. Ibid., p. 223.
28. See Pierre Macherey, *A Theory of Literary Production* (London, 2006), p. 128.
29. Ernst Gombrich, *Art and Illusion* (London, 1992), p. 56.
30. Northrop Frye, *Anatomy of Criticism* (Princeton, NJ, 1957), p. 132.
31. Ibid., p. 75.
32. Rachel Bowlby, 'Foreword', in Beaumont (ed.), *Adventures in Realism*, p. xvii.
33. Ibid., p. 59.
34. Frye, *Anatomy of Criticism*, p. 136.
35. See Catherine Belsey, *Critical Practice* (London, 1980), especially Ch. 4. For a perceptive critique of Belsey's case see Penny Boumelha, 'Realism and Feminism', in Furst (ed.), *Realism*. See also Colin MacCabe, 'Realism and the Cinema', *Screen* (Summer, 1974) for an argument to which Belsey is avowedly indebted.
36. Roland Barthes, *Mythologies* (London, 1972), p. 199.
37. Roland Barthes, *Writing Degree Zero* (New York, 1967), pp. 67–8.
38. Friedrich Nietzsche, *The Gay Science* (New York and Toronto, 1974), para. 355.
39. Thomas Hobbes, *Leviathian* (Cambridge, 2010), p. 175.
40. Fredric Jameson, *The Ideologies of Theory* (London, 2009), p. 420.
41. Fredric Jameson, *The Antinomies of Realism* (London, 2013), pp. 215 and 5.
42. See John Brenkman, 'Innovation: Notes on Nihilism and the Aesthetics of the Novel', in Franco Moretti (ed.), *The Novel*, vol. 2: *Forms and Themes* (Princeton, NJ, and Oxford, 2006), p. 811.
43. Franco Moretti, *The Way of the World* (London, 1987), pp. 52 and 54.

3 WHAT IS REALISM? (2)

1. Matthew Beaumont, 'Introduction: Reclaiming Realism', in Beaumont (ed.), *Adventures in Realism*, p. 4.
2. Henry James, 'The Art of Fiction', in Morris Shapira (ed.), *Henry James: Selected Literary Criticism* (Harmondsworth, 1963), p. 80.
3. Northrop Frye, *Fables of Identity: Studies in Poetic Mythology* (New York, 1963), p. 36.
4. Jameson, *The Ideologies of Theory*, p. 420.
5. Levin, *The Gates of Horn*, p. 24.
6. See Jameson, *The Ideologies of Theory*, p. 422 ff.
7. Ibid., p. 422.

8. Raymond Williams, *The English Novel from Dickens to Lawrence* (London, 1970), p. 116.
9. Raymond Williams, *The Long Revolution* (Westport, CT, 1961), p. 287.
10. See Roland Barthes, 'The Reality Effect', in *The Rustle of Language* (New York, 1986), p. 143.

4 THE POLITICS OF REALISM

1. See M.H. Carré, *Realists and Nominalists* (Oxford, 1946), and D.M. Armstrong, *Universals and Scientific Realism*, vol. 1: *Nominalism and Realism* (Cambridge, 1978).
2. Charles Taylor, *A Secular Age* (Cambridge, MA, and London, 2007), p. 94.
3. See C.B. MacPherson, *The Political Theory of Possessive Individualism* (Oxford, 1962).
4. See Terry Eagleton, *The Ideology of the Aesthetic* (Oxford, 1990), Ch. 1.
5. Michael Polanyi, *The Tacit Dimension* (Chicago, IL, 1966), p. 19. See also Maurice Merleau-Ponty, *The Phenomenology of Perception* (London, 1962), pp. 4–5.
6. Some of Johnson's remarks on these matters can be found in W.J. Bate (ed.), *Samuel Johnson: Essays from the* Rambler, Adventurer, *and* Idler (New Haven, CT, and London, 1968).
7. Jameson, *The Ideologies of Theory*, p. 437.
8. György Lukács, *Studies in European Realism* (London, 1972), p. 194.
9. György Lukács, *The Meaning of Contemporary Realism* (London, 2006), p. 68.
10. Lukács, *Essays on Realism*, p. 130.
11. See Ferenc Fehér, 'Lukács in Weimar', in Agnes Heller (ed.), *Lukács Revalued* (Oxford, 1983), p. 96.
12. Quoted in George Bisztray, *Marxist Models of Literary Realism* (New York, 1978), p. 112.
13. *Soviet Writers' Congress, 1934* (London, 1977), p. 7. For useful studies of Soviet aesthetics, see Herman Ermolaev, *Soviet Literary Theories 1917–1943* (New York, 1977); Brandon Taylor, *Art and Literature under the Bolsheviks*, 2 vols (London, 1991 & 1992); and Boris Groys, *The Total Art of Stalinism* (New Haven, CT, and London, 1992).
14. Quoted in Bisztray, p. 115.
15. *Soviet Writers' Congress, 1934*, p. 135.
16. Ibid., p. 150.
17. Ibid., p. 124.

18. Ibid., p. 248.
19. Ibid., p. 89.
20. Quoted by Becker (ed.), *Documents of Modern Literary Realism*, p. 197.
21. Quoted by Raymond Williams, *Keywords* (Oxford, 2015), p. 199.
22. Quoted by Becker (ed.), *Documents of Modern Literary Realism*, p. 207.
23. Lukács, *Studies in European Realism*, p. 149.
24. See Lilian R. Furst and Peter N. Skrine, *Naturalism* (London, 1971), p. 47.
25. For a taste of Lukács's hostility to naturalist art, see his essay 'Reportage or Portrayal?' in Lukács, *Essays on Realism*, as well as his essay on Émile Zola in *Studies in European Realism*.
26. Émile Zola, 'The Experimental Novel', in Becker (ed.), *Documents of Modern Literary Realism*, p. 171.
27. Erich Auerbach, *Mimesis: The Representation of Reality in Western Literature* (Princeton, NJ, 2003), p. 490.
28. Quoted by Levin, *The Gates of Horn*, p. 71.
29. Jacques Rancière, *The Politics of Literature* (Cambridge, 2011), p. 8.
30. William Dean Howells, 'Criticism and Fiction', in Donald Pizer and Christopher K. Lohmann (eds), *W.D. Howells: Selected Literary Criticism*, vol. 2: *1869–1886* (Bloomington and Indianapolis, IN, 1993), pp. 302–3.
31. Theodor Adorno, *The Culture Industry* (London, 2001), p. 182.
32. Quoted by Williams, *Keywords*, p. 163.
33. Sally Ledger, 'Naturalism: "Dirt and Horror Pure and Simple"', in Beaumont (ed.), *Adventures in Realism*, p. 77.
34. See Becker (ed.), *Documents of Modern Literary Realism*, p. 238.
35. 'The nineteenth-century dislike of Realism is the rage of Caliban seeing his own face in a glass. The nineteenth-century dislike of Romanticism is the rage of Caliban not seeing his own face in a glass': Preface, *The Picture of Dorian Gray*, in Terry Eagleton (ed.), *Oscar Wilde: Plays, Prose Writings and Poems* (London, 1991), p. 69.
36. Marcel Proust, *Remembrance of Things Past*, vol. 2 (New York, 1932), p. 1009.
37. Linda Dowling (ed.), *Oscar Wilde: The Soul of Man under Socialism and Selected Critical Prose* (London, 2001), p. 167.
38. Ibid., p. 184.
39. Ibid., p. 187.
40. Ibid., p. 191.
41. Ernst Bloch et al., *Aesthetics and Politics* (London, 1977), p. 47.
42. Ibid., p. 76.

43. Ibid., p. 81.
44. Ibid., p. 77.
45. Ibid., p. 66.
46. Ibid., p. 81.
47. Quoted in Lilian Furst (ed.), *Realism*, p. 34.
48. Quoted in George Bisztray, *Marxist Models of Literary Realism* (New York, 1978), p. 174.
49. Levin, *The Gates of Horn*, p. 83.
50. See Briony Fer, David Batchelor and Paul Wood, *Realism, Rationalism, Surrealism* (New Haven, CT, and London, 1993), p. 254.
51. Lois Boe Hyslop and Francis E. Hyslop (eds), *Baudelaire as a Literary Critic: Selected Essays* (University Park, PA, 1964), pp. 87–8.

5 REALISM AND THE COMMON LIFE

1. Moretti, *The Way of the World*, p. 11.
2. Mikhail Bakhtin, *The Dialogical Imagination: Four Essays*, ed. Michael Holquist (Austin, TX, 1981), p. 259.
3. Charles Taylor, *Sources of the Self* (Cambridge, 1994), p. 211.
4. Ibid., p. 213.
5. Auerbach, *Mimesis*, p. 22. Further references to this work are provided in parentheses after quotations. For a valuable survey of Auerbach's life and work, see Geoffrey Green, *Literary Criticism and the Structures of History* (Lincoln, NE, 1982), Part 1.
6. Edward Said, 'Introduction', in Auerbach, *Mimesis*, p. 5.
7. Shapira (ed.), *Henry James*, pp. 86–7.
8. Quoted by Habib, *History of Literary Criticism*, p. 474.
9. On taking the common life seriously, see Stanley Cavell, *In Quest of the Ordinary* (Chicago, IL, and London, 1988).

INDEX

abstraction 103–4, 109–10, 115, 140–3
achievement and desire 10–11
Acts of the Apostles 132
Adam Bede (George Eliot) 2, 58, 133
Adorno, Theodor 110, 121
Aeschylus 111
aesthetics
  Adorno on realism 121
  Auerbach on Rabelais 138
  Brecht on 127
  Hegel on 106
  invention of the modern 103
  Lukács on modernism 109
  the sublime 80
Alice in Wonderland (Lewis Carroll) 41
alternative viewpoints 4
American New Critics 110
Amis, Martin 38
Anderson, Perry 127
Animal Farm (George Orwell) 64
animals 13

Appiah, Kwame Anthony 21
Aristotle 4, 104, 110
art
  bourgeoisie 114
  Brecht 127
  clarity of realist art 80
  communicating universal truths 104
  Dickens and 34
  the general and the particular 104
  a heritage of high art 111
  Iris Murdoch on 30
  mirrors as 58–9
  modernist art 66, 86, 109, 110
  naturalism 121
  Nietzsche 129
  non- (or anti) realist art 60, 78
  Oscar Wilde on 124
  photography and 117
  Plato's suspicions of 59
  procedures adoptable 126
  realism and the common people 132, 141

realist art's problem (or illusion)
    8, 51, 80
representational art 63
Soviet Union 112
specific historical conditions
    and 111
T.S. Eliot on 37
Auden, W.H. 114
Auerbach, Eric 42, 119, 132,
    134–42
Austen, Jane 3, 42, 85, 92, 96–7

Bakhtin, Mikhail 132, 142–3
Balzac, Honoré de
    Engels admires 29
    English perceptions of 32
    Lukács on 106, 107–8
    non-realism within 33
    realism in 73, 139
    social forces beneath the politics
        75
bankers 20
Barthes, Roland 67, 97, 98
Baudelaire, Charles 130
Beaumont, Matthew 79
Beckett, Samuel 99, 109
Belsey, Catherine 67, 69
Bennett, Arnold 45, 116
Berkeley, George 144
Bible, the 4, 17, 97–8, 132–5
Blackburn, Simon 19, 25
Blake, William 80
Blanchot, Maurice 6
Bleak House (Charles Dickens) 33,
    34, 80
Borges, Jorge Luis 78
bourgeoisie 38–9, 107–9, 114,
    116 see also middle classes
Bowlby, Rachel 62
Brecht, Bertolt 66, 78, 125–8

Brenkman, John 74
Breton, André 36
Britain 10, 70, 76
Bukharin, Nikolai 115
Bull, Malcolm 22

Calamity Jane 63
Cambodia 8
Camera Lucida (Roland Barthes)
    98
Camus, Albert 109
Canterbury Tales (Geoffrey
    Chaucer) 43
Cantos, The (Ezra Pound) 110
capitalism
    Adorno on 110
    fragmentation and opacity 108,
        143
    Hardy's capitalist economy 92
    lack of order and stability 72,
        145
    Marx on capitalists 39
    realist art as an alternative 106
    transition of in West 145
Cat in the Hat, The (Bo Welch)
    63
Cézanne, Paul 74, 129
characters
    biblical 134
    capitalism and 145
    Defoe's 40
    Dickens's 34
    evolving over time 35
    inner world of, and outer
        context of lives 3–4, 96
    modernism 109
    non-realist fiction 60
    omniscient narrators and 66
    realism and naturalism 117, 123
    Shakespeare 139

socialism and 126
   Victorians 50
Chartists 75
Chaucer, Geoffrey 43
China 13
choice 12–13, 74
Christianity 8, 99, 132–5, 137 *see
   also* Bible; God; Jesus
   Christ
class antagonism 30
climate change 23
Clooney, George 65
closure (in novels)
   classic realism 68
   D.H. Lawrence 88
   Defoe's novels 40
   drawing the line 72
   Jane Eyre and Nabokov 81
   middle-class problem with 40
cognitive realism 24
coincidence 34, 65, 104
Coleridge, Samuel Taylor 36, 41,
   117
commodity 110
common threads through different
   societies 22
Commune (Paris) 122
communism 105, 127
Communist Manifesto, The
   (Friedrich Engels and Karl
   Marx) 38, 74
concepts 53, 100–4
consciousness 30–1, 45–6, 114, 116
consensus 19
Constructivism 59, 127
context 3, 5, 16, 44
Courbet, Gustave 122
Creation 99
critical realism
   decline of 108

deviating from 116
   Lukács's terminology 107,
      140–1
   naturalism and 121
   postmodernism and 144
   proletarians and 113, 115
   subject and object 118–19
Cruise, Tom 63
Cubism 66

Dadaism 59, 127
Dante Alighieri 138, 140
Darth Vader (*Star Wars*) 13
Darwin, Charles 123
David Copperfield (Charles
   Dickens) 48
Davison, Donald 22
Death of a Salesman (Arthur
   Miller) 136
'Decay of Lying, The' (Oscar
   Wilde) 124
Defoe, Daniel 35, 40, 73
desire 12, 40
desire and achievement 10–11
desire and oblivion 46
desire and social convention 97
Dickens, Charles 30, 33–5, 73, 80
Disraeli, Benjamin 75
diversity 19, 21
Divine Comedy, The (Dante
   Alighieri) 63, 140
Don Quixote (Miguel Cervantes)
   38–9, 42, 51
Dostoevsky, Fyodor 64, 73
Dracula (Bram Stoker) 64
Dreiser, Theodore 116

East Germany 128
Easter Rising (1916) 76
Egdon Heath 71

ego, the 30, 48
Eliot, George
    Adam Bede 2, 58, 133
    history as progress and 83
    Middlemarch 3, 29, 76
    morality and 4
    naturalism and 123
    one of the first godless novelists
        94
    as realist novelist 33, 75
Eliot, T.S. 37, 42, 110, 114
Emerson, Ralph Waldo 117–18
Emma (Jane Austen) 85
emotivism 26
empathy 5, 8
empiricism
    fiction and 52
    from medieval to modern 143
    middle classes 39
    nature of 2
    the sensible and the rational 103
Engels, Friedrich 29
Enlightenment, the 6, 71
'Enoch Arden' (Alfred Lord
        Tennyson) 43
epic literature 3, 37–8, 134–5
epistemology 28, 31, 84
equity (Aristotelian) 4
ethics, systems of 5, 26, 28, 133
Euripides 111
Expressionism 125

facts 11–15
    cognitive realism and 24
    feelings and 4–5
    leavenings of fiction 9
    moral facts 27
    values and 26, 28
Far from the Madding Crowd
        (Thomas Hardy) 91, 95

Farewell to Arms, A (Ernest
        Hemingway) 64
fascism 107, 114, 140
feminism 16, 75, 95
Fernandez, Ramon 85
Fielding, Henry 35, 86
first-person narration 66
First World War 108
Flaubert, Gustave
    banal yet fastidious 64
    Madame Bovary 122
    naturalism 116
    quote from a critic 120
    realism in 139
football 8–9
Forestry Commission 71
Forster, E.M. 70
France
    naturalism 93
    realism's associations 33, 36,
        111, 140
Freud, Sigmund 46, 48
Frye, Northrop 60, 65, 80
Futurism 127

Galsworthy, John 45, 116
Garaudy, Roger 129
Garcia Marquez, Gabriel 65
Gaskell, Elizabeth 30, 96
general and the specific, the 102,
        104
Germany 103
Ghosts (Henrik Ibsen) 122
Gissing, George 73, 116
global capitalism *see* capitalism
God 80, 102, 133–4
Goethe, Johann Wolfgang von 29,
        140
Gombrich, Ernst 60, 61, 62
Goncourt brothers 116, 120

INDEX

goodness 29–30
Gorky, Maxim 114, 115
Great Expectations (Charles Dickens) 34
Greece (ancient) 111
Gulliver's Travels (Jonathan Swift) 43–4, 64, 65

Habib, M.A.R. 32
Hardy, Thomas 88–95
  ambiguities of 93
  challenging received versions of reality 73
  from the trivial to the tragic 120
  history in the time of 83
  importance of work in 92
  Jude the Obscure 33, 92–5
  one of the first godless novelists 94
  Return of the Native, The 70–1, 88–91, 94
Hare, R.M. 148
Hegel, Georg Wilhelm Friedrich
  a lineage of moralists 28
  Lukács influenced by 106
  Marx influenced by 107
  naturalism in Hegelian terms 121
  particulars 144
Hemingway, Ernest 64
Historical Novel, The (György Lukács) 106
history
  legend and 135
  Lukác's position 107–10
  middle classes in 38, 74
  passion for the particular as a landmark 102
  of realism as a narrative form 38, 86

  of representation 60
  of science 17–18
  the shape of 83
History and Class Consciousness (György Lukács) 105
Hobbes, Thomas 70
Homer 134, 135
Horace 43
Howells, William Dean 120
Hungarian Soviet Republic 105
Hungary 128

Ibsen, Henrik 75, 116, 122
'Idea of Order at Key West, The' (Wallace Stevens) 85
ideology 67, 70
If These Apples Should Fall (T.J. Clark) 74
Immaculate Conception 70
India 70
individuals
  modernism 109–10
  naturalism 119
  postmodernism 18
  priority given to over the universal 35, 37, 103
  realist art's depictions 106
  Reformation 134
  social convention and 96, 103
  socialism 112
interpretation 11–12, 14, 68
Ireland 76
Irish Times 76
Italian Journey (Johann Wolfgang von Goethe) 29

Jacobins 75
Jakobson, Roman 43
James, Henry
  'the air of reality . . .' 143

INDEX

on *L'Assommoir* 122
morality and 4
'The Real Thing' 54–7
'The Story in It' 36
on Trollope 79
turning point in realism 33
Jameson, Fredric 73–5
'desacralising' social reality 87
realism as illusion 84
'representation of reality' 41
suppressing the fiction in realist
fiction 51
Jane Eyre (Charlotte Brontë) 81,
97
Jesus Christ 97–8, 132–3, 135
Job, Book of 93
John, St (the Apostle) 132
Johnson, Samuel 73, 104, 105,
125
Joyce, James
Auerbach on 139
realist and modernist 109
Ulysses 44, 64, 115
Jude the Obscure (Thomas Hardy)
33, 92–5

Kafka, Franz 64, 86, 109
Kane, Sarah 75
Kant, Immanuel 28
King Lear (William Shakespeare)
44
Kingsley, Charles 30
Kissinger, Henry 8
kitchen sink drama 123
knowledge
art and 30
cognitive realism 24
context and historically set 16
moral knowledge 27, 28
nominalism and 102

political emancipation 23
realism and 26
values, beliefs and 12

Lady Chatterley's Lover
(D.H. Lawrence) 4
language 32, 53, 62, 66–7
Larkin, Philip 42
Larry's Party (Carol Shields) 9
L'Assommoir (Émile Zola) 123
Lawrence, D.H. 4, 88, 95–6
Lazarus 98
Lenin, Vladimir 58
Levin, Harry 37, 129
Lewes, G.H. 128
liberal democracy 70
literary realism *see* realism
Little Dorrit (Charles Dickens) 73
London 122
London, Jack 116
Lord of the Flies (William Golding)
84
Lovibond, Sabina 12, 27
Lukács, György 105–12
Auerbach and 136, 140–1
Brecht on 125–6
on naturalism 118, 121, 124–5
realism and political action 31
socialist realism and 115–16
two senses of realism 128
Luke, Gospel according to 133
lyric fiction 3, 51
Lyrical Ballads (Samuel Taylor
Coleridge and William
Wordsworth) 36, 41, 117

Macbeth (William Shakespeare)
49, 102
Machery, Pierre 58–9
MacIntyre, Alasdair 27

INDEX

Madame Bovary (Gustave Flaubert)
  122
magic realism 65–6
Malevich, Kazimir 59
Mann, Thomas 107
Marx, Karl
  Communist Manifesto 38–9, 74
  influence on of Hegel and
    others 107
  the particular 144
  typicality with individuality 106
Marxism 106, 107, 111
Mary Magdalene 98
Matthew, Gospel according to 135
Maupassant, Guy de 51, 116
Mayor of Casterbridge, The
  (Thomas Hardy) 91, 92
McEwan, Ian 113
*Meaning of Contemporary Realism,
  The* (György Lukács) 112
Medea (Euripides) 111
Melville, Herman 75
Metamorphosis (Franz Kafka) 86–7
'Michael' (William Wordsworth)
  43
Mickey Mouse 63
Middle Ages 100–1
middle classes 37–40
  atheism and 94
  and the birth of literary realism
    132
  decline of 108
  European 143
  Gorky's view of 114
  Hardy's novels 92
  history and 74
  humanism of 107
  naturalism 121–3
  problems with order and closure
    40

Protestant ethic 133
realism and 32–3
revolution and 77
stripping illusions of fable and
  romance 87
truth and 23
Middlemarch (George Eliot) 3, 29,
  76
Mill, John Stuart 21
Milton, John 16
*Mimesis: The Representation of
  Reality in Western Literature*
  (Erich Auerbach) 134,
  136, 137, 140
mirrors 58–9
Moby Dick (Herman Melville) 84
modernism 107–10
  examples of technique 66
  Lukács's hostility 112
  naturalism and 125
  realism anticipates 42–3
Moll Flanders (Daniel Defoe) 35
monarchy 70
Mondrian, Piet 142
money 40–1
montage 66
Montaigne, Michel de 137
morality 26–31
  Appiah on 21
  base for values and beliefs 12
  naturalism 119–23
  realism qualifying 4
  realism's moral values 39
  virtuous action 28
Moretti, Franco 76, 131
Morris, William 77
Mrs Dalloway (Virginia Woolf) 44
Mulhall, Stephen 26
Murdoch, Iris 4, 29–30, 103
Musil, Robert 109

Nabokov, Vladimir 78, 81
Nagel, Thomas 24
naturalism 93, 112, 114–25
Nature 70–3, 92, 118–19, 146
Nazis 129, 140
New Objectivity 129
New Testament 97, 133, 140
New Women 95
News from Nowhere (William
    Morris) 76
Nietzsche, Friedrich 11–12, 14,
    68, 129
Nightingale, Florence 9
nihilism 14
1968 riots, Paris 6
nominalism 100–3
non-realist art
    Auerbach on 139
    Brecht 127
    creation of 60
    in language and content 64
    moral truth and 27
    political views and 78
    realism's debt to 88
    realistic and non-realist 130
    within realist art 33
Norris, Christopher 24
North and South (Elizabeth
    Gaskell) 96
Northern Ireland 6
novels
    Clara Reeve on the novel's
        highest task 7–8
    'once upon a time' 78
    realist novels
        assimilation of other forms
            by 86
        chance turning into necessity
            99
        confining the definition 65

conservative nature of? 68,
    69–70, 75–6
contingency and necessity 97,
    99
depictions of revolution 76–7
diversity and density of 75
form and content not always
    both realist 64
innocence of 67
Lukács on 106
marriage in 96–7
as mirrors 58
and morality 4, 30
most unliterary of literary
    art 51
need for editing 80, 82
no independent existence
    outside the novel 49
Protestant ethic leading to
    133–4
puncturing illusions of fable
    and romance 87
real-life characters and facts
    in 52
rules for reproducing 60–2
style sacrificed to substance 79
that touch of bad faith 42
various faults of 67–8
verisimilitude and 84

objectivity
    desire and 12
    moral truth and 27
    naturalism
    New Objectivity 129
    realism and 4
    self-centredness and 29
O'Grady, Paul 25, 147 n14
Oliver Twist (Charles Dickens) 34,
    93–4

omniscient narrators 66
On Liberty (John Stuart Mill) 21
Othello (William Shakespeare)
46–7
Oxford English Dictionary 6

Paine, Thomas 71
Pamela (Samuel Richardson)
35, 38
Paris 6, 122
particulars 36, 97, 100–4, 144
Paul, St 98
perception 12, 24, 29, 34
Persuasion (Jane Austen) 3
Peter, St 98, 132
Petrarch 60
Phidias 129
Philosophical Investigations (Ludwig
Wittgenstein) 20, 59
philosophy 1–2, 28, 48
photography 117
Picasso, Pablo 129
Pierce, C.S. 14
Plato 28, 59, 141
pleasure principle 48
Pnin (Vladimir Nabokov) 81
Polanyi, Michael 104
Pope, Alexander 134
positivism 13
postmodernism
    aversion to natural world 71
    knowledge and context 16
    modernism and 42
    parameters of realism and 9
    realism's fate in 144–6
    right wing and 17
    scepticism re the settled and the
        rooted 72
    scepticism towards science 25–6
    seeing things as they are 11

similarity of other cultures and
    21
truth and 17–18
wariness of facts 13
Pound, Ezra 78, 110
Poussin, Nicolas 129
prescriptivism 148 n20
Pride and Prejudice (Jane Austen)
    68
proletarian art 113–15 *see also*
    working classes
Protestant ethic 133–4
Proust, Marcel 8, 45, 109, 124
Prowse, David 13
psychoanalytic theory 46–7
Puritans 36
Putin, Vladimir 23
Putnam, Hilary 18

Rabelais, François 138
Racine, Jean 134
Radek, Karl 114–15
Rainbow, The (D.H. Lawrence)
    96
Ravenna 129
'Real Thing, The' (Henry James)
    54–7
realism
    Auerbach on, a summary
        139–40
    Brecht and Lukács 126
    cognitive realism 24
    conflicting views on nature
        of 43–4
    critical realism 107, 108, 115,
        119
    critiques and re-creations 5,
        36–7
    definitions 33
    described 32–3

excess reality, an artist's problem
        55–6
    imaginative transformation and
        57
    in a postmodern age 144
    meaning of in everyday
        language 1
    Middle Ages 100–1
    middle-class origins 37–8
    moral realism 27–9
    mutability and 74–5
    realistic and 7, 130
    regarded as scandalous and
        indecent 33
    revolution and 76–7
    socialist realism 112–15
    starting points and timescales
        33, 42
    surface appearance and hidden
        depth 145
    two features of fiction 35
    two senses of 128
    within other forms of writing 43
    word enters English language 32
reality
    and the concrete particular 103
    a definition 14–15
    falling short of expectations 9
    internal and external 45
    language and 53
    the mystical and 80
    order within it 57
    in psychoanalytic theory 46
    rough and ready pre-artistic
        structure of 62
    social change and 103
    as verisimilitude 65
    a world independent of us 48
Reeve, Clara 8
Reformation 134

relativism
    avoidance of consensus 19
    a definition 15
    foisted on to other cultures 22
    group relativism 20
    sending up 18
    Relativism (Paul O'Grady) 147
        n14
Renaissance 111
representation
    fidelity and image 7
    history of 60
    literary works as 59
    Mimesis 137
    Nazis 129
    not a simple concept 53–5
    realism and 41, 63, 65, 68, 126
    reflection and 58
    truth and 128
restraint 11
Resurrection, the 8
Return of the Native, The (Thomas
        Hardy) 70–1, 88–91, 94
Révai, József 110
Richardson, Samuel 35, 38
right-wing positions 17
Rights of Man, The (Thomas Paine)
        71
Rise of the Novel, The (Ian Watt) 35
Roman Catholic Church 70
romantic literature 38, 97,
        117–18
Romanticism 102, 120, 142, 152
        n35
Rorty, Richard 14, 148 n19
Rushdie, Salman 113
Russia 74
Russian Association of Proletarian
        Writers (RAPP) 113
Russian revolution (1905) 58

INDEX

Said, Edward 140
science
  art and 117
  errors as much as discoveries
    16–17
  exchanging hypotheses 16
  methods 12
  naturalism 118
  postmodernists' scepticism 25
  religion and 102
Scott, Walter 42, 75, 107, 111
Scruton, Roger 26
Sebald, W.G. 49
Sense and Sensibility (Jane Austen)
    17
Shakespeare, William
  limits to his realism 139
  Lukács on 106
  Macbeth 49
  Othello 46
  realism's heritage and 111
  Troilus and Cressida 10
  Winter's Tale, The 46–7
Shaw, George Bernard 116
Sheen, Charlie 7
Shelbourne Hotel, Dublin 76
Sholokhov, Mikhail 115
Simonyan, Margarita 23
Sinclair, Upton 116
situations 103
  Balzac 108
  concept and 103
  Lyrical Ballads 36
  realism and 51, 96, 99
  representations of 54
  Zola on 117
slave trade 6
'Snow White and the Seven
    Dwarfs' (Brothers
    Grimm) 78

soap operas 69
Social Darwinism 123
socialism 112–16
  characters evolving 126
  Courbet 122
  Lukács on 107
  William Morris 77
Sons and Lovers (D.H. Lawrence)
    95
Sophocles 134
Soviet Union 112–13, 129
Soviet Writers' Congress (1934)
    113, 115
Stalinism 105, 112, 141, 143
Stendhal 36, 73, 112, 139
Sterne, Laurence 83
Stevens, Wallace 85
Stoicism 1
Stoker, Bram 64
'Story in It, The' (Henry James) 36
Streetcar Named Desire, A
    (Tennessee Williams) 66
Strindberg, August 116
Studies in European Realism
    (György Lukács) 106
Surrealism 66, 125, 127
Swift, Jonathan 43
symbols 80, 87–9, 96, 104

Taylor, Charles 13, 102, 133
'Teddy Bears' Picnic, The' (Jimmy
    Kennedy) 51
Tempest, The (William
    Shakespeare) 64
Tennyson, Alfred Lord 43
Tess of the d'Urbervilles (Thomas
    Hardy) 73, 92
tolerance 3, 4–5, 70, 89
Tolstoy, Leo 58, 107, 111, 123
Tolstoy, Nikolai 113

Tom Jones (Henry Fielding) 35, 86
transformation
    art and 57
    human nature and history 101
    non-realism 2
    postmodernism 145
    revolutions 76
    socialist realism 114
    Zola 30
Tristram Shandy (Laurence Sterne) 83
Troilus and Cressida (William Shakespeare) 10
Trollope, Anthony 75, 79
truth 16–21
    art and 8
    cognitive realism 24
    communicating universal truths 104
    conflicting narratives 23
    etymology 28
    existence of 14
    middle classes and 23
    modernism 66
    morality and 27
    naturalism 118
    non-realists and 27
    not mere fidelity to fact 57
    only realism gets to 126–8
    postmodernism and 16, 67
    Proust 45
    psychoanalysis and 47
    to be discovered not constructed 25
Turgenev, Ivan 75

Ulysses (James Joyce) 44, 64, 115
Under the Greenwood Tree (Thomas Hardy) 92
Under the Net (Iris Murdoch) 103

United States 10, 36, 75
urban art 34
utopian fiction 75

value judgments 16
values 20–2, 26–8
    knowledge and moral value 30
    moral thinkers 12
    middle classes 39, 132
    naturalism 119
    Protestant ethic 133
    value judgments 16, 26, 31
Vattimo, Gianni 11
verisimilitude 65, 81, 84
Victorians 50, 73, 93–4, 94–5
Virgin Mary 70

Waiting for Godot (Samuel Beckett) 129, 141
'Walrus and the Carpenter, The' (Lewis Carroll) 51
Waste Land, The (T.S. Eliot) 110
Watt, Ian 35
Waverley (Walter Scott) 111
weapons of mass destruction 23
Weber, Max 87
Wells, H.G. 45, 116
Where the Wild Things Are (Maurice Sendak) 129
Whigs 140
Wilde, Oscar 123, 124
Williams, Raymond 92, 96
Williams, Tennessee 66
Winter's Tale, The (William Shakespeare) 46–7
wisdom 1–2, 69, 102, 142
Wittgenstein, Ludwig 11, 20, 59
women 18, 23, 98
Women in Love (D.H. Lawrence) 96

Woodlanders, The (Thomas Hardy)
   92
Woolf, Virginia 44–5, 78, 95, 139
Wordsworth, William 36, 41, 43,
   117
working classes 75, 94, 108–9, 114
Wuthering Heights (Emily Brontë)
   16, 50

Žižek, Slavoj 60
Zola, Émile 117–19
   challenging received versions of
      realism 73
   English criticism of 122
   L'Assommoir 123
   naturalism 116
   purpose of writing 30